DARTS

(1709)

£8
1980
VG/VG
DES

DARTS

Keith Turner

Foreword by Tony Brown
and drawings by John Henry

DAVID & CHARLES
NEWTON ABBOT LONDON NORTH POMFRET (VT)

For Su

British Library Cataloguing in Publication Data

Turner, Keith
  Darts.
  1. Darts (Game)
  I. Title
  794   GV1565

ISBN 0–7153–7943–7

Library of Congress Catalog Card Number
79-56063

Photoset by
Northern Phototypesetting Co Bolton Lancs.
Printed in Great Britain
by Redwood Burn Ltd. Trowbridge Wilts.
for David & Charles (Publishers) Limited
Brunel House Newton Abbot Devon

Published in the United States of America
by David & Charles Inc
North Pomfret Vermont 05053 USA

Contents

Part IV   The evolution of darts

Upon the wall opposite the open fireplace there was a board, marked out as a sun-dial, each division bearing the value of some number. A ring in the centre marked the highest number of all. The board was painted black, and all about the face of it were little holes where darts had entered. It was a game they played to wile away a lazy hour.

At Eynsham Harry's invitation, we played with them then – played for four glasses of ale, while the landlord in his apron leaned within the doorway, keeping the score with a piece of chalk, pleasantly content whoever won or lost.

(E. Temple Thurston, *The "Flower of Gloster"*, 1911)

Foreword

One minute nobody has heard of Tony Brown and the next I am rated number two darts player in the world. How did it all happen? This is a question I am often asked by darts fans all over the country, including youngsters hoping they have the potential to break into the professional ranks when the time comes, and by seasoned players knowing in their hearts they are good enough but needing that break at the right time.

I first started playing the game in 1956 when my father decided to take a public house, the Falcon Hotel, in Dover. I was eleven at the time and this gave me an early opportunity to play darts. I think that in any sport the earlier you are able to participate the more advantageous it is, provided, of course, you possess that natural ability which is required to succeed at the highest level. I can remember very clearly how I would rush home from school, change out of my uniform, push my homework aside and go into the bar to practise. Often I would need a stool to reach the darts above the double top. The Falcon Hotel has long since been pulled down to make way for road improvements but every time I cross the road where it used to be I think to myself, 'this is where it all started'. What if my father had not become a licensee? Would I have ended up playing darts? I doubt it.

I mentioned earlier that the younger you are when you start playing a sport, the easier it is for you. Well, I had a cricket bat shoved in my hand from about two years old and so my childhood ambition was to play county cricket for a living. My father and his four brothers had all played professional cricket or football so I suppose it was only natural for me to have a similar ambition.

However, we took another pub, the Three Cups, in 1960. I was now fifteen and did not require the stool anymore. Homework was still being neglected but I was doing well at cricket and football at school. I started chalking for the local darts team and was fortunate at this stage to be able to mix with good players and learn the right shots to throw for. This is a very important aspect in darts, especially at top level, where every dart counts. To know automatically what to throw for when you require a finish is a great asset because you do not have to hesitate and risk losing concentration.

By the time I was seventeen, I was playing in the first team at the Cups and occasionally winning local titles. My cricket, too, had gone well and I had joined Dover Cricket Club where I was adjusting to a higher class of club cricket. At twenty years of age, I was given the opportunity to join the Kent Club and Ground Staff, but unfortunately due to work I was unable to attend regularly and the chance dwindled. However, in the games I did play I performed well, and held my own with several of the lads who are the backbone of the present county team.

Meanwhile, I was becoming a more prominent figure in local darts, and once I had realised that my chance of playing professional cricket had slipped away, darts gradually began to take over from cricket. In January 1973, the British Darts Organisation was formed and an inter-counties league soon followed. As most counties had not formed a super league by this time, there was no way county secretaries could examine results and scores to determine their leading players, so many of them arranged friendlies with other counties hoping that a galaxy of local talent would emerge. Kent officials decided to stage a match between the north and south thus giving them a chance to see in action players from both ends of the county, from which they could select the basis of their forthcoming county team. Having been successful at this time by winning several local titles, I was selected to represent South Kent in this intriguing fixture. I was drawn out first and although I gave a good account of myself, I was narrowly beaten by two legs to one. However, I must have shown the selectors that I had the potential to become a county player because shortly afterwards I was selected to play for the Kent first team.

I will always remember my first game. It was played at Crayford Social Club against Surrey who at the time were a very strong side. I was drawn out about fourth and scored very well but failed to get my doubles to finish, a fate that seems to befall a lot of youngsters making their county debuts. Probably a case of being a little nervous and trying too hard. After my game I remember going to the back of the hall to sit down and watch the rest of the matches. I had been sitting there about ten minutes when Tom Barrett, that gentleman of darts who won the *News of the World* two years running, came over and sat beside me. He obviously thought I looked disheartened and wanted to cheer me up. What a marvellous gesture by such a great player to come and talk to a disappointed youngster, knowing I needed a few words of encouragement at that time. This is the type of person who has helped to put darts where it is today, and I know that myself and several other players who are doing well at the moment can look back and realise what we owe to the pioneers of yesterday.

Well, Tom and I had a chat about several aspects of the game, and by the time we had finished it was surprising how much better and reassured I felt. Tom went off to play his game, which I watched admiringly, hoping that one day I would emulate this great sportsman.

There is an incredible difference playing in your local against average players and playing in front of up to five hundred spectators against a top player from another county. There are about four different progressive stages in darts, each one producing higher-class opposition and requiring greater concentration and experience to succeed. The first is obviously playing in your local in leagues or cup matches. The second is playing in your super league team which should produce most of the best players in your area. The third is being selected for your county and the fourth, the ultimate, becoming an England International. I believe that each of these different stages requires at least a year at that level before you produce the darts that you are capable of throwing. In other words, you require a year to adjust to the different pressures and tensions that each progressive step produces.

I was probably just as good a dart thrower ten years ago. It is just that now I have become more experienced by playing in front of large audiences and against top players most of the time. Becoming number two in the world does not just happen. You have to spend a lot of time and money besides being one hundred per cent dedicated and producing maximum effort all the time. I suggest entering all tournaments that you can to give you the chance to play against top players from other parts of the country, thus building up your experience. You will not improve by playing in your own back yard all the time, and beating players inferior in ability to you.

I finished the rest of the season with the Kent A team and found that I won about as many as I had lost. Not a record to shout about but enough to suggest I could hold my own at county standards given enough time. My record the following year helped to change my destination in life and eventually to become a darts professional. I went through the whole season without losing a game and this was the stepping stone to becoming a full England International. My name was submitted to the England selectors and after scrutinising my county performances, they decided I had earned my chance to represent my country.

I was selected to play against Wales at Tottenham in May 1976. Once again I had a good game but was just pipped by three games to two. This time I did not feel too despondent because I had given a good account of myself and was pleased with my performance, although of course I would have preferred to have started with a victory! My international career progressed and I found that, as in my first county season, I was winning one and losing one. There was no magic formula for instant success, only hard work, endeavour and persistance. I find now that at international level I am producing the form and getting the results I know I am capable of. So, I must again stress to players progressing to a higher standard of darts, give yourselves a year before judging your performances. Don't give up and think that the standard is too high for you. Remember, I took a year at each level to produce the form that I was capable of. I'm glad I didn't give in.

Even though I have had the good fortune to reach the top of my profession and now travel all over the world, whenever I am at home I still call in at the local to have a game and chat with the lads. After all, this is where I started on my long trail to darting fame. I often look back and think how much we owe to darts secretaries everywhere who have formed leagues and given up their own time to organise and help run competitions, all of which help the local players to improve.

There is no doubt that the sport of darts holds a certain fascination for all of the millions who endeavour to play, from the average pub thrower to the top professionals.

I often compare it with golf in that one day you can go round the course in a respectable score and the next you are struggling to get round in under one hundred. Yet, there is no apparent explanation. With darts you can throw a perfect hundred followed by twenty six, and in your own mind, the darts have been held exactly the same and released in the same way.

To try and achieve a nine dart leg, the minimum possible at 501, is a target which holds a certain amount of fascination, especially for the top players. For the average player, progress may be measured by counting the number of darts required to finish a leg of 501. Starting, say, at 30 darts, improvement may be seen when they break 25 darts and then 20 darts until they near perfection by throwing 15 darts and under. Also, what an achievement to throw three darts into the treble twenty or into the inner bull for someone who has never done it before. Probably fifty per cent of all darts players will never reach such figures, so all their lives they will be a challenge.

The appeal the game has to the general public is tremendous. Darts has no physical barriers — housewives and school children are equally capable of hitting that elusive target. They all have three darts in their hands and it is up to the individual how they throw them.

I feel, personally, there is an aura of magnetism about the game, an excitement at getting the winning double whether it is a top professional adding another title to his credit, or an average player winning the knockout at his local. Because the cameras are able to get so close, darts is a natural for television. Viewers are able to see the expressions made by players, a look of satisfaction or of disappointment. Also, people who cannot find time to attend top darts competitions can understand why the sport has such spectator appeal because the game is played at a fast pace with a quick build-up to the final climax.

So, all in all, darts has a fascination and appeal that is not generated by many other sports and I am sure that with the help of the media, especially colour television, it will become one of the most popular games of all time.

In the following pages I feel that the author has produced a book which is a must for anyone wishing to improve their knowledge of darts as well as their performance. A lot of interesting data has been accumulated, together with many useful tips, which has created an ideal balance in producing a narrative of real value.

Happy darting

Tony Brown

Part I: The basics

1 The rules

Chapter 1 is intended for newcomers to the game and may
be skipped by more experienced players unless guidance on
a specific point of dispute is sought.

The first point about the game is that there is no one definitive set
of rules for darts: different rules apply in different places and in
different competitions. But there are a number of principles
basic to the various forms of the two-player standard game and
these are outlined below; elaborations of specific details are given
in the following chapter.

The set-up

1 The game is between two players, each of whom has three
   darts.
2 The players throw their darts at the dartboard from a
   position behind the hockey or toe-mark.
3 If a player oversteps the hockey with any part of his foot
   whilst throwing a dart any score made by that dart does not
   count.
4 At each turn, the player throws his three darts.

Order of play

5 Order of play is decided either by the toss of a coin or by
  'bulling-off': each player throws one dart at the dartboard
  and the player nearest the bull starts the game. If the darts
  both land in the same value bull, or are equidistant from it,
  they are removed and rethrown.

The start

6 The player winning the toss or nearest the bull takes first throw.
7 A player must hit a double before he can start scoring.
8 A player's first double counts as his first scoring dart.
NB: If a 'straight start' game is being played then Rules 7 and 8 do not count. Instead, a player's first dart is his first scoring dart.

Scoring

9 A player's starting score is 301, except in a 'straight start' game when it is usually 501.
10 The total points scored during a throw are subtracted from 301 in the case of his first scoring throw and thereafter from his previous total.
11 Darts that land off the board, bounce out, fall out before being removed by the player, fail to reach the board or stick into another dart do not score.
12 Darts dropped before or during a throw can be rethrown.
13 A dart's score is determined by the numbered area of the board into which the point of the dart sticks, according to the wire boundaries of the various areas.
14 The score of a throw is only determined after all three darts have been thrown (except under Rule 16).

The finish

15 A player must hit a double to finish the game.
16 The finishing double must be the exact value of the player's remaining score after his previous throw.
17 The 50 bull counts as a double.
18 If a player takes his score down to 1 or less without hitting a finishing double then that throw is over and the score does not count.
19 The player wins the game by first reaching 0.

Pairs play

Pairs play is subject to the same general principles as the two-person game but the scores of the partners are added together. Play is alternate: one player from one team, one from the other and so on. Starting score is usually 501 in friendly games.

If a double start is played then normally only one player from each team needs hit it, though in some areas both players are required to do so.

2 The standard game

At the beginning of the first chapter it was noted that the game of darts is played in different ways in different places. Developing the rules already given, this chapter explains in detail just how the standard game and its several variations are played.

The London board

Also known as the Clock, Treble or No 1 board (I have

Fig 1 The London board

deliberately avoided calling it the 'standard board'), this is the modern board as used widely throughout Britain and the world for all major, national and international competitions. As its name indicates, its main stronghold was London though its use has now spread far beyond that city.

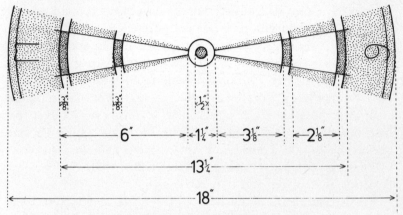

Fig 2 London board dimensions

The London board is a circular target (*see* Fig 1) some 18in in diameter and divided up into various 'beds' by a web of thin wires (the 'spider') stapled to the surface; these beds each have their own value and so form the different scoring areas. In the very centre is a circular bed $\frac{1}{2}$in across: the inner bull scoring 50. Around the inner bull is a second circle, $1\frac{1}{4}$in in diameter: the outer bull scoring 25. From the outer bull twenty equal-area segments radiate like the spokes of a wheel and these are numbered (clockwise) from the top: 20, 1, 18, 4, 13, 6, 10, 15, 2, 17, 3, 19, 7, 16, 8, 11, 14, 9, 12 and 5. The total scoring area is $13\frac{1}{4}$in in diameter and the rest of the board to the edge is a non-scoring area and merely serves to carry the segment numbers and to provide a soft landing for stray darts. A second ring of wire inside the outer limit forms the 'doubles' beds for each segment and darts landing here score double that number. A similar ring midway between the doubles ring and the bull makes up the 'trebles' and darts here score three times their face value. The overall diameter of the treble ring is $8\frac{1}{4}$in. (*See* Fig 2.)

The face of the board is normally coloured black for the non-scoring area with the various beds filled in with a two-tone colour scheme in a symmetrically contrasting manner – usually black and yellow or black and white. The better boards also employ green and red for the alternate doubles and trebles which makes the whole effect far less harsh on the eyes. The segment numbers themselves are either painted directly onto the surround, in the case of cheaper boards, or made from bent wire on a 'numbers ring' around the edge; wire is also used to delineate the beds so as to avoid any argument over the position and score of a dart. Cheaper boards are commonly made from a strip of tightly-wound paper like a huge ticket roll, or from cork or some modern composite material. Even plasticine is sometimes used. But the best boards are fashioned from elm or from tightly-packed bristles which take a dart better and with less damage. This type of board is generally thicker (at about 2in) than the cheaper varieties, is stronger and will last longer.

Bristle boards are manufactured from sisal fibres from East Africa rather than animal bristles and these are first packed into brown paper tubes in a machine which churns them out like long sausages. The tubes are then cut into slices and fifty or so of these are then compressed into a solid disc the size of the dartboard and banded with a metal strip, with a breaking strain of some ten tons, to hold them firmly in place. Each board, on average, contains about sixteen million fibres. The colours are then screen-printed on and the spider added; single-sided boards are bonded onto a backboard.

CARE AND MAINTENANCE
The better quality the board, the longer it will last if properly looked after. Wherever possible obtain one that can be turned in relation to its mounting so that it can be rotated regularly and the number ring correspondingly turned to even out the wear on the number 20. Such a feature is often found only on the more expensive boards – another reason for buying the best. A reversible board (one with a face on both sides) is of course of added value though for practise at home virtually any sort of board will do.

Even the best board, if played on lunchtimes and evenings, day after day, will begin to show the strain after a matter of months and if it is of the bristle variety it will tend to disintegrate in really spectacular fashion with bits bulging out all over the place.

Never soak a non-wooden board in order to soften it.

Positioning of the board

The board should be hung in a vertical position on a wall with the centre of the bull 5ft 8in above floor level. (Manchester and Kent boards are generally hung 2in lower.) It is positioned so that the 20 segment, in the case of London-numbered boards, is at the top and the 3 segment vertically below it. Though optional, boards are invariably surrounded with some form of protection for the wall such as a wooden cabinet, half a car tyre, or even both.

A strong lamp should be positioned to direct its light onto the board; if mounted, as is usual, above the board it should be sufficiently high to be out of the way of the darts – though in some pubs such fittings are unfamiliar hazards for visitors! It should also be shielded to protect the bulb and to prevent it shining into players' eyes.

The hockey

The hockey or toe-line is the mark laid down on the floor from behind which players have to throw. Any dart thrown from in front of the hockey, with the player's foot at least partly over the line, should be declared non-scoring by the scorer. It usually takes one of two forms: either a wooden or metal strip fastened to the floor or a line on a rubber mat stretching to the board. The latter type also serves to protect the floor from the countless pairs of feet trudging up and down it; they are normally supplied by the brewery to the pub or club in question.

The British Darts Organisation does not use the word 'hockey' any longer, preferring 'oche' which it claims is an Anglo-Saxon word meaning a groove in the floor or ground from which archers shot. The plain truth is that 'oche' is not Anglo-Saxon at all but archaic English owing its origin to the Old French meaning to nick or notch. It is probably the ancestor of 'hockey' but should the traditional terminology of the game be altered to provide spurious evidence to try to support dubious claims about the game's ancestry?

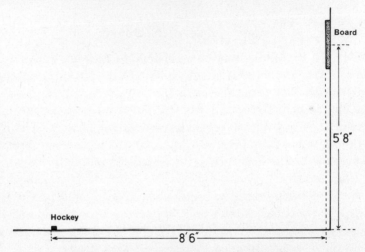

Fig 3 The set-up using an 8ft 6in hockey

The positioning of the hockey is determined by measuring from the perpendicular of the wall on which the board is mounted (*see* Fig 3); the actual distance is subject to considerable regional variation. Depending upon local rules and customs, the throwing distance can be anything between 6ft and 9ft in steps of 6in. I have tried to perceive some sort of pattern in the geographical distribution of these different throwing distances, but to no avail. One of the problems is that they have altered over the years as leagues were set up and, as the circles of competition widened, so more and more pubs adopted a convenient mean. My own theory is that at first the hockey was simply placed a suitable distance from the board so that throws were not too difficult yet not too easy. Of paramount importance were purely local considerations – the game had to be accommodated within the space available! Small bars would tend to produce short hockeys; the tiny fishing pubs of Yarmouth gave rise to 6ft marks whilst the grander drinking halls of the Midlands could safely contain 9ft or more. The record is possibly the 10ft hockey noted by Croft-Cooke at Kingham in Oxfordshire. To complicate matters still further, some old marks have been laid down by measuring with a string (eg 8ft long) from the bull itself to the floor, making for a decidedly odd length of throw!

The *News of the World* competition has adopted the 8ft hockey as the standard for its Area, Division and Grand Finals (players can of course stand further back than this if they so wish), but the choice is left to local practice for the early heats. The most common lengths are probably 8ft or 8ft 6in although for televised matches this is usually brought down to 7ft 6in to produce more spectacular shots. One advantage of using a mat to mark the hockey is that it often has a choice of lines on it – eg 8ft, 8ft 6in and 9ft. In mixed friendly games women are customarily allowed to stand 6in closer to the board than men.

The width of the hockey should be 3ft but the width is really immaterial anyway since, in theory, the hockey extends indefinitely on either side. So a player, if he wishes, can throw from next to the wall on the other side of the room, providing he is standing behind this imaginary extension of the line.

Scoring

The keeping of the score is traditionally done on a slate or blackboard, with white chalk, beside or close to the dartboard. Modern innovations such as white plastic sheets and coloured-ink markers are ugly, messy, harder to clean (and read) and altogether no substitute for the smell and dust of the real thing! A damp cloth is usually to be found lying about somewhere at hand to wipe the slate clean between games.

The purpose of the scoreboard is to provide a visual record of each side's score and to avoid any dispute on the subject. The normal fashion of doing this is to set out each side's score down one half of the board, with a real or imaginary line between them; traditionally the side that starts scoring first takes the left-hand side of the board. The game score, 301 or whatever, is usually written over the top. (*See* Fig 4.) Crossing out previous

scores is optional. For a more serious level of play, scoreboards
are used which have two columns per side: one for the score left

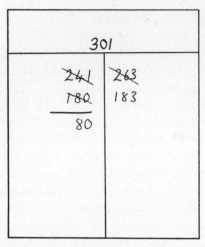

Fig 4 301 scoreboard; the player on the right is about to throw

and one for the score of each throw. This provides a double check
on the accuracy of the marking with every throw recorded in
black and white. (*See* Fig 5.)

Over the years a form of shorthand has developed for use
during scoring. While numbers such as 264 are written in full,
100 or 200 are usually represented as 1— or 2— etc; similarly
205 is shown as 2–5, 108 as 1–8 etc. Doubles are normally
written 20x, 16x etc – and if say 20x is split (only a single 20 is
hit) to leave a player with double 10, then all the scorer has to do
is simply rub out the x to leave 20 on the board. A shot of 100 is
commemorated with a line below the previous score (*see* Fig 4);
further variations are the use of B (for bull) for 50 and Tx (for
double top) for 40.

A variation more common in the north of England is the use of
automatic scorers. These are fiendish mechanical devices hung
on the wall in place of the normal scoreboard. At the beginning
of the game they are set to display 301 or whatever for each
player or side. (They come, like trouser legs, in pairs.) Any score
then made is dialled into the thing by means of a telephone-like
dial below each digit, thus automatically subtracting the score

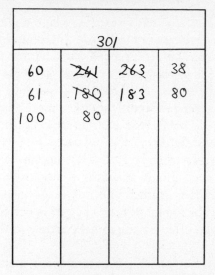

Fig 5 301 scored as in match play

and displaying the new total. My own experience with these objects has left me decidedly wary of them since every time I have tried to use one it had a very good go at my fingers. It is also impossible to score other games on them; the scoreboard has to be equally versatile as the dartboard itself.

Who then does the scoring? Practically gone for ever are the days when the landlord would perform this necessary task 'pleasantly content whoever won or lost'. Nowadays the players have to do it themselves – unless you are lucky enough to discover some remote pub one lunchtime with no one in it except you, the landlord and his dog. If, however, someone has 'got his name up' then the problem is solved for the task is performed for you. This widespread convention consists of a person who wishes to play a game initialling the scoreboard for the privilege of scoring the next game and then playing its winner. In a busy pub there might well be a whole string of initials waiting their turn. In other words, a successful player stays on the board while successive opponents score his games before playing him. It is, in effect, a challenge which the player receiving it is duty-bound to accept.

As in most other games the final decision in case of any

disagreement should be left to the person in charge: the scorer. He should also advise players who are uncertain as to which side of a wire a dart has landed and call out what has been scored so far if asked. He is *not* however expected to advise a player as to what he should aim for or tell him what score he has left in the middle of a turn. Since a significant part of the game involves the working out of the best possible targets and finishes, such advice is unsporting and unfair to the opposing player. This point is often overlooked in friendly games but how many darts scorers would, for instance, dream of telling a snooker player what ball to go for if refereeing a game? The only exception to this rule is in the case of a doubles game where a player is perfectly entitled to consult with, and offer advice to his partner in the middle of a throw.

In major tournaments, matches and exhibitions, another type of scoreboard is used in conjunction with the traditional one. This takes the form of a large representation of a dartboard fitted with three electric light bulbs in each bed (the singles have two in the large and one in the small beds); a second scorer plugs the corresponding sockets on a smaller, matching board in front of him according to where the darts have landed at each throw. The result is that spectators in the body of the hall where the game is being played, with no hope of seeing where the darts actually hit, are given a clear visual indication of each shot. (I am reminded by this of a tale overheard in one of my former lunchtime locals. Two old gaffers were reminiscing about darts in general when one said: 'You remember old Fred? Got to the *News of the World* final in 1935 – or was it 1936? Anyway, after all that sitting about waiting to throw, he was on his thirteenth pint when he went to the board.' The old fellow supped his drink reflectively. 'Didn't win, though.' I imagine old Fred had no hope of seeing where his darts actually landed either.)

Such tournaments also have a 'checker' to call out the shot for the benefit of the chalker who keeps the actual score.

THE CRIBBAGE BOARD
It should be noted in passing that for certain games a cribbage board is traditionally used for scoring purposes. (See Chapter 9

for details of these.) Since the card game of crib or cribbage has been played in pubs since the seventeenth century it is hardly surprising that the two games are linked in this close manner.

The invention of cribbage is attributed to Sir John Suckling

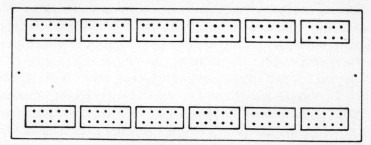

Fig 6 Cribbage board

(1609-42), a noted poet, womaniser, rake, courtier and gambler. It was not an entirely new game but an adaption of an older game called Noddy and used a similar board for scoring. This contains two rows of thirty holes down each side (ie two lines per player) and a single game hole at either end. Thus just once up the board is 31 while up and down is 61. (*See* Fig 6.) Crib boards are also used for scoring certain other pub games (notably dominoes) and, being far older than darts, were no doubt adopted for scoring the first, simple versions of the latter game.

301

At its simplest, the standard game is known as '301' or '301-up' and is for two players. Each throws for the bull or tosses a coin, as explained in the Rules, in order to decide who starts the game. It is an important advantage to be the first to throw in the game proper.

The player opening the game then throws his three darts in turn at the board, attempting to hit any double. As soon as he succeeds, he can throw to score anywhere on the board. The value of the starting double and successive scores are subtracted from 301 and marked on the scoreboard as described in the previous chapter: eg double 6 away, treble 20 and a single 20 scores 92, leaving 209 on the scoreboard. (Throughout the remainder of this book double 6 or whatever will be written as 6x and treble 20 or whatever as 20t.)

The second player then throws his three darts, then the first player again and so on, each pushing their total scores along as quickly as possible until they are in a position to 'get out' – end the game. This has to be done by hitting the double to eliminate his score so any even score of 40 or under will suffice – as also in fact will the 50 bull. For example, if a player is left with 30, a dart in the 15x bed will win him the game. If however he hits the single 15, he now has 15 left and must score an odd low number so as to leave himself a chance at another double. If a player scores too many, 'going bust', so that he more than wipes out his score, then his whole turn is ignored and he reverts to his previous score. For example, if a player is left with 38 and hits a single 19 instead of the double with his first dart and hits it again with his second (while going for the 3 to leave himself 8x), then he is bust. His throw ends and next time around he tries again from 38. (Note that he does not have to try for 38 as his finishing double: he is perfectly entitled to go for any combination that suits him eg 6 – 16x.)

At one time though it seems that the general rule was that if a player went bust he reverted to the very last score aimed for, whether it was in the middle of a turn or not. Thus in our example, after the two single 19s the player in question reverts to 19, not 38. The argument for this rule was that if a player made a mess of an easy double and left himself, say, 3, he could not deliberately bust it by a high scoring shot and so have another crack at the easy double. The argument against it is of course that if a player wishes to throw away his turn, then he has already penalised himself by virtue of the fact that his opponent has been allowed, in effect, an extra throw. A word of warning though: if playing in a strange place make sure which rule is followed there. I well remember playing in a friendly doubles match in a Derbyshire village and causing not a little amusement, firstly by standing a good foot behind their short hockey and secondly by going for different doubles from my partner!

In 1977, the national social club body, the Club and Institute Union, introduced 'levelling-up' into its national tournaments (some areas had been playing this way for years); some people would like to see it adopted elsewhere as well. Under this rule, the second player is allowed as many darts as the first in order to win or draw the game. For example, if the first player wins on his eighteenth dart then his opponent, who has only thrown fifteen darts so far, is allowed an extra throw of three; finishing on the sixteenth or seventeenth would give him the game, finishing on the eighteenth would draw it. To me, this is not how darts should be played since by playing over a number of legs (eg the best of three or five games), the advantage given by starting first is shared. Besides, with the traditional 'first one out is the winner' system, an unequivocal, positive result is always reached.

Variations can be made on the basic 301. '301 straight off' is played without the necessity to score a starting double. The game can also be played as a foursome between two pairs, turns alternating between players from opposing sides, or with three or four players playing individually, though this is not so enjoyable as team play.

Finally, in the Manchester area (and perhaps elsewhere) a local variation is that players must finish on their starting double – a far trickier game altogether.

501

This is traditionally the game for two pairs and is much the same as 301 except that the starting score is 501. Either member of a team can start scoring by hitting a double (though in some places there is a local rule that *both* players in a team have to hit one). It is also played as '501 straight off' in major competitions between two individuals and is seen in this form in televised games. It certainly makes for a fiercer game than 301 as both players are racing down to that final double from the start.

Other variations

1,001 can be played as either a change from the usual game or as a contest between two teams, thus giving each player a fair number of turns at the board. 3,001 makes for a nice lunchtime marathon — as I well remember from sweltering strawberry picking days in a delightful Cambridgeshire pub — but only if no one else wants a game! Longer games are normally reserved for endurance records (sometimes farcical), fund raising and the like. In these events 1,000,001 is the usual target.

101 and 201 make excellent practice for keeping players on their toes since 101 can be all over in just three darts and 201 in four! A recent introduction (recent at least to my knowledge) is 801 straight off as a team game with three players a side; 401 will be met with in some pubs as the accepted pairs game because, being shorter than 501, it generally allows more people to have a chance of a game during the course of an evening. Although personally I have never witnessed a game of 601, 701, or 901, doubtless these variations too have their own ardent supporters.

3 Traditions and conventions

We have seen that the standard game of darts, together with its variations, is played in accordance with the basic principles outlined in the previous chapters. There are, however, a number of traditions and conventions which surround the game; these 'unofficial rules' have grown up over the years and are to be met with in some shape or form wherever the game is played. So be warned!

Traditional throws

The term 'traditional throws' is given to those special throws which are permitted only on special occasions. They are *not* allowed in match or tournament play, only in friendly games – and only then if both sides agree on the matter. The normal procedure is that when the opportunity for such a throw arises the player wishing to make it will ask if his opponent(s) will accept it; if it is accepted then the result of that throw is binding upon the game.

There are six of these traditional throws in widespread usage and, while local variations do exist, the fundamentals of each are set out below. The first two can be used at almost any time during the game, the third only on certain occasions and the last three at the very end of the game.

SHANGHAI
Perhaps the most widely known of the traditional throws, this is a shot of three darts with one in the single bed, one in the double and one in the treble of the same number. According to local custom the darts *must* be landed in either single, double, treble or single, treble, double order. The shot should be requested after the first two darts have been thrown when only the double or the treble remains to be hit. If accepted by the other side and the

throw is successful and Shanghai is achieved, the player wins the game outright; if he fails in his bid then the score from those three darts is not counted and the game proceeds in the normal fashion.

The risks involved must be weighed by both sides. Obviously a failed Shanghai on 20 is far more damaging to the challenger's score than on 1 – but is more likely to be accepted by opponents for that very reason!

THREE IN A BED

The other 'anytime' shot is three in a bed – all three darts in the same double or treble bed. (Though often requested, singles do not count!) As with Shanghai this shot has to be asked for before the third dart is thrown and the outcome is the same: a straight win or loss of score for that turn.

TREBLE 1 ETC

This is a shot which can only be used rarely, unless it is deliberately played for, which is most unlikely. If a player is left with a score of 111, he can nominate to score 1t with the first dart of his turn. If he hits it then the game is over and he has won; if he misses then his throw is at an end and any score made is ignored. Similar throws can be used for 222 (2t), 333 (3t) and 444 (4t) when playing 501.

SPLITTING THE 11

This is the best known of the three 'finishing throws'. It is used when a player throws for 1x to get out and instead hits the single. If he has any darts left in that turn he is allowed one throw at the figure 11 on the edge of the board in an attempt to land the dart between the wire legs of the numeral and so win the game.

This shot is normally accepted only when both sides are throwing for 1x.

THREE FOR IT

When stuck on 1x, both sides can agree to throw 'three for it' – all three darts are thrown regardless of whether any of them score elsewhere. The player who originally began the game is the first to throw in this manner when his turn comes round. The first player to hit 1x wins the game.

THROWING FOR THE BULL
Used when things get really desperate! The two players (or one from each side when playing in pairs) each throw one dart for the bull, the player who started the game throwing first when his turn comes round. The dart nearest the bull wins the game just as that nearest the bull started it.

Local conventions

From the above and the previous chapter it should be clear that darts is played in very different ways in different places. Mention has been made of the accepted convention of marking a game before playing one. Other local conventions might however replace this particular one or add perculiarities of their own. The only safe advice is that when not on home ground respect the local way of doing things. It is only polite to do so – and extremely prudent!

Another, different, widespread convention is often found in the form of a note by the board to the effect that scores of a certain shamefulness (eg 11 or under) warrant a penny or so in the bar's charity box. This definitely adds a touch of concentration to even the friendliest of games!

Finally, a word of warning: if playing a strange convention for the first time, *do* make sure that you understand it properly. There is the cautionary tale of a man on holiday in the West Country who found himself one evening playing darts in the village pub. He was down to his finishing double when his opponent, still needing a hundred or more, suddenly threw a 13, a 17 and a 1. Whereupon the scorer wiped the scoreboard clean and started the next game. The stranger, being naturally somewhat perplexed by this odd turn of events, asked what had happened. 'Oh, Walter got a zum-doodle,' said the scorer. 'Wins the game, does a zum-doodle,' he continued in response to the stranger's blank look. He pointed to a small notice high up in one corner of the far wall: '13-17-1 ZUM-DOODLE WINS THE GAME'.

'I see,' responded the stranger and sat down. When his turn at the board came round again he decided that this was an easy way to win and promptly threw a zum-doodle of his own. Walter carried on as though nothing had happened. 'Hey', cried our stranger, 'I've won! 13-17-1 zum-doodle wins the game!'

'Sorry,' replied the scorer, pointing to an even smaller notice behind the bar: ONLY ONE ZUM-DOODLE PER NIGHT.

Part II: *Winning play*

4 Your darts

Their history

Details of the very earliest darts are obscure but it seems highly probable that the first successful darts were of a type not unknown even today, though vanishing rapidly. The main body of the dart was made of wood turned or carved into a streamlined cigar shape. At the blunt end a drilled hole took the metal point while at the other end was fitted a three-feather flight. A band of lead set into the centre of the body provided the weight to carry the dart through the air.

It would be difficult to conceive of a simpler form of construction, except perhaps for using an unshaped dowel for the body which the earliest darts possibly did. It was fairly easy to make and simple though it was, it was certainly not primitive. In the hands of an expert it is still as good as most designs and better than many but there were however two basic drawbacks to it. Firstly, it was on the bulky side and to land three in a treble bed was well-nigh impossible. The second drawback was that you could buy a dart of any weight and size providing you wanted this (rather light) standard! Model T Fords may or may not all have been black; wooden darts were certainly identical from the one manufacturer. (*See* Fig 7 for a typical example.)

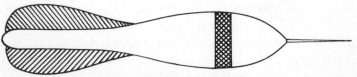

Fig 7 Pre-war wooden dart

35

It did not take long for players with inventive minds to apply themselves to the task of producing a dart just better than the other fellow's and no doubt amongst the serious players whittling and weighting was all the rage. The first major advance from the traditional dart came in 1898 when the folded paper flight was patented in America. It was undoubtedly a revolution in dart design for it meant that a damaged flight could be swiftly and cheaply replaced without having to throw the whole dart away – and, more importantly, it heralded the idea of the custom-made dart.

Others were quick to explore the possibilities now open to them. In 1900, a patent was taken out in Britain for the simple metal clip round the body, just below the flight, to hold paper flights securely in place (the old style feather ones were glued into the body rather than slotted in). It was followed six years later by the detachable metal barrel, and the idea of a dart individually tailored to suit the player, not the manufacturer, had arrived.

The next development was the introduction of the celluloid flight, the forerunner of the modern plastic ones now used. The possibilities of this material had in fact been known since the nineteenth century and it was a logical, more durable, substitute for paper. Collapsible like the paper ones, these new flights had the great advantage of outwearing their flimsier rivals. Then, just before World War II, came the next step: metal shafts that would not split or splinter like the cane ones which carried the flights. Made of aluminium alloy for lightness, and screwing into the barrel instead of being just a push-fit, their invention is credited to one Frank Lowy – appropriately enough a patent agent and consulting engineer – who went on to found Unicorn Products Ltd, one of the leading names in the post-war boom in darts equipment. Another of Lowy's major innovations was to sell his darts in sets of three, instead of the old practice of retailing them in a loose assortment, and his outlets were sports shops rather than the general hardware stores which stocked the wooden ones. Though now taken for granted, such a move was at the time revolutionary and of immense importance in raising the status of the game during the 1940s.

Since then this pattern of dart has almost completely displaced the wooden variety, though they do still have their individual adherents and pockets of local use. One of my memories of the 1950s and early 1960s is that their last stronghold in my locality was in the visiting fairs where 'Three darts a tanner! Over 60 or under 21 wins a prize!' could be heard from nearly every other stall. And with the rough, blunt and ragged darts offered, that was no mean feat! Now they too have gone plastic – though the warped flights and blunt points still retain some link with the past.

The modern dart

Almost all darts used today are of the type shown in Fig 8. Although variations exist between the styles and designs of different manufacturers, the basic features are much the same.

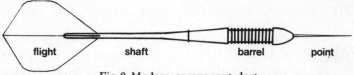

flight   shaft   barrel   point

Fig 8 Modern component dart

The dart can be divided into four separate components – separate that is by function though not necessarily physically so. These four parts are: the *point*, the *barrel*, the *shaft* and the *flight*.

The *point* is the business end of the dart, 1in or less in length and made of high tensile steel for durability. Ground to a sharp tip, it enables the dart to stick firmly in the board without the weight making it drop out.

The *barrel* is also made of metal, into which the point is permanently embedded, and is commonly made of turned brass for cheapness and easy machining – though heavier metals such as nickel-silver or tungsten alloys are increasingly being used. This section is anything from 1½–3in or so long and is provided with a machined grip over at least part of its length to ensure a firm grasp of the dart between the finger tips. The weight of the barrel (anything between the common limits of 12-42g) supplies the weight to carry the dart to the board and to sink the point into it. There are three basic barrel shapes: straight, barrel and torpedo (*see* Fig 9). The first has an even distribution of weight down its length, the second has the weight concentrated in the centre and the third has it towards the front.

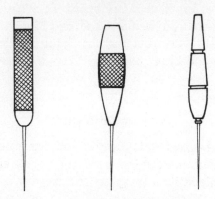

Fig 9 The basic barrel shapes: (Left to right) straight, barrel and torpedo

The *shaft* comprises the remainder of the body of the dart and is usually proportioned to the barrel and point to bring the total length of the dart to between 4-6in. It is detachable from the barrel normally by a screw-thread, though if of wood then it is merely wedged in, to allow replacement if bent or otherwise damaged. Materials used are cane (now going out of fashion as it tends to split and splay out very quickly), aluminium alloy (for lightness) or a plastic compound; these are the firm favourites even though a number of other substances, both dull and esoteric, have been, and are being, experimented with. Like the point and barrel it is circular in cross-section for aerodynamic balance. Its function is to hold the flight the correct distance away from the barrel.

The *flight* is the rear end of the dart and provides the stabilizing influence needed to keep the point facing forward in the air. Enormous variations exist in both the design of the flight and the material from which it is made. Traditionally it comprises three or four feathers embedded in the shaft in symmetrical fashion. The highest quality ones are made from the leading wing feathers of a turkey; only two from each wing are used. Split down the quill, they provided eight flight feathers – less than one set of darts! A cheaper substitute is synthetic ones but they are not nearly so fine. There is perhaps a tendency today to dismiss such old-fashioned equipment out of hand and advocate the latest multi-coloured plastic fin. It should however be remembered that, despite their size, feather flights possess two distinct advantages. To begin with, they are the only type of flight that can let another dart pass *through*. If a feather flight blocks the treble 20 bed, there is no obstacle whereas all other types of flight will, to some degree or other, deflect anything hitting them. Its second great advantage is that, if of good quality, each feather in the flight will be naturally curved in relation to the shaft (*see* Fig 10). This feature of the feather means that when the dart is thrown, the flight imparts a slight spin to it which improves the accuracy of its passage through the air, just as the rifling on a gun barrel does to a bullet.

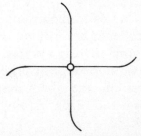

Fig 10 End-on view of a feather flight

The second-best type of flight is the paper variety. Bought as a flat, curiously shaped piece of stiff paper, gummed on one side, it is wetted with spit (or, to really impress your opponents, with the top off your beer) and folded into a four-finned shape ready for slotting into the end of the shaft. A poor third comes the modern plastic or nylon horror. Although these deflect other darts more than paper ones (they are much less flexible), it should be said in their favour that they too fold flat when not in use and are therefore convenient to carry. A small point in favour of both paper and plastic flights is that they provide less than half the drag through the air of feathers; this is because feather flights are corrugated whereas paper and plastic are smooth.

Design and development

The point excepted, the designer of a modern dart enjoys considerable latitude. He has however to work within certain limits imposed by three ruling factors: weight, size and aerodynamic stability. Naturally all three factors are closely interrelated and any decision affecting one must also be considered in terms of the other two.

The weight of the dart can vary considerably between the rough limits of 12-42g. The preferred weight is very much an individual matter and has to be taken into account by the darts manufacturer in the form of a whole range of barrels of different weights. There are two basic ways of doing this still using the same design: increasing the size of the barrel or altering its composition. So to produce heavier brass barrels, the width has to increase but by using another material, such as a much denser tungsten alloy, the same weight can be achieved within a far slimmer barrel.

The size of the dart is vitally important: it must be possible to land all three darts in a treble bed without recourse to wide-angle shots, and this means that there is a practical limit on the width of the barrel. This used to be a great problem for players who preferred a heavy dart but since the widespread availability of tungsten alloy barrels in the 1970s this obstacle has largely been overcome. (See below.)

As regards the length of the dart, it is commonly somewhere between 4in and 6in although the generally accepted upper limit is getting on for 7in. This is really a size of convenience more than anything else (there is no rule to say that you can't throw 3ft darts if you want to) and has evolved from the normal practice of throwing the dart from close to the eye. Longer darts would pose serious hazards when trying to sight down them! At the other extreme are miniature darts an inch or so in length, sold as novelties rather than for competition. Although I once played a skilled exponent of the art of throwing these diminutive objects, they are only novelties and lack the weight needed for most people to throw them accurately – and to make them stick in the board. Half-size darts, which are exactly that, are occasionally seen but they cannot be obtained in the same quality as full-sized ones. Their lack of weight is also a problem. On the other hand, extra long darts suffer from the problem of too much weight and tend to drop out of the board after hitting it.

The factor ruling the overall design of the dart is aerodynamic stability. This governs the proportions of the dart and the design of its flight. The barrel must be around the centre of gravity and the flight must have enough surface area to ensure that the point is kept facing forward in the air. The heavier the dart, the larger the surface of flight needed to counterbalance the weight of the barrel. Conversely, the further back from the barrel the flight is set, the smaller it can be to provide the same balance. If the flight is too small in relation to the weight, it simply will not work and the dart will tend to turn sideways in the air – as it will if the barrel (and centre of gravity) is set too far back. For the same reason the flight must be balanced in relation to the shaft so that any sideways motion in any direction is checked; in practice this means three or four feathers/fins positioned equidistant from each other around the shaft. The whole battle is to supply just enough stability to make the dart fly true whilst keeping the flight size down to a minimum to avoid blocking out following darts.

The tungsten revolution

Tungsten has provided the biggest revolution in dart design since the war. First experimented with in the early 1960s by aircraft engineers in the Bristol area, the possibilities of the new material were recognized by dart manufacturers and the market for such darts tested in the mid-1960s. As a set retailed for at least ten times the price of brass darts, it was by no means certain that they would sell in appreciable quantities. It transpired that there was in fact a good demand for them and during the 1970s it has become increasingly rare to see a professional player using any other kind.

Since the words 'tungsten darts' are used without qualification by a few manufacturers and many retailers, some explanation is called for. Tungsten itself is an exceptionally dense, hard and brittle metal and whilst the first quality makes it an ideal possibility for dart barrels, the other two do not since a rod of the metal in its pure state would be extremely difficult to machine and prone to snap anyway when subjected to any degree of stress. Pure tungsten has a density of $19.3g/cm^3$ which makes it more than twice as heavy as brass for the same volume – or, to put it another way, a weight of tungsten would occupy less than half the space needed for the same weight of brass. Hence its attraction as a material for dart barrels. The problem of working the metal is overcome by alloying it with either copper (density $8.9g/cm^3$) or nickel ($8.8g/cm^3$) or both. (Both these other metals are themselves denser than brass.)

The amounts of the different elements used to make the final alloys vary widely and this affects the cost and size of the product. The cheapest 'tungsten darts' on the market contain a lot less than 70% tungsten and more than 30% copper while the most expensive contain over 90% tungsten. The more tungsten, the denser the dart; the more copper, the less dense it will be – and the more likely to tarnish due to a reaction with the acids present in perspiration from the fingers. The better quality manufacturers add nickel, a more expensive metal than copper, to prevent this happening.

The safest path through this jungle of statistics and prices is to be willing to pay for the best and to make certain that you know exactly what you are getting. Only buy darts which are accompanied by a note or certificate of how much tungsten they do in fact contain. A certificate for a good set should carry the following typical information:

Material specification
Tungsten (99.9% purity) 90%±1%
Nickel/copper   10%±1%
Density
$16.8g/cm^3 \pm 0.2g/cm^3$
Weight
21.6g

Otherwise you are not only likely to be paying over the odds but paying too much for a poor product.

Is it all worth it? The only true answer is that that is for you to decide. Tungsten alloy darts will not magically make you throw any better if you already have a good set of arrows; what they will do is make finer shots possible and give you chances that did not exist before. And there is also the added bonus of the confidence you obtain from the knowledge that they are the best darts currently available. If you are happy with 12g brass 'nails' there would be little to be gained by switching; if however you need 40g 'bombs' then a tungsten set at that weight could make a world of difference to your game.

Future trends

Quite obviously, the modern dart has not yet reached its final design stage and probably never will. Ideally a dart should be as thin as its point all the way down and with no flight! That appears to be impossible in both theory and practice but it remains the goal and new ideas continually appear on the market in an attempt to overcome at least some of the problems inherent in the present design.

The dart point is the area in which the least change is likely. Perhaps one day someone will bring out a dart that never needs sharpening but apart from that there appears to be little or no scope for improvement. As for the barrel, new designs are regularly being tested. The obvious possibility is that new (and inevitably highly expensive) materials will be utilised in the quest for even denser, slimmer barrels. On a more mundane level there is still a lot that can be done with regard to grip patterns and weight distribution. (One firm even produces a hollow barrel with a sliding weight inside that can be set to suit the individual player.)

Without doubt the majority of experiments currently underway are those concentrating on the shaft/flight arrangement and the obstacle it presents to other darts. These are often tested on the market and either survive as worthwhile or disappear as mere gimickry. One recent idea is to fit a metal deflector cap to the shaft (either on the end or halfway down the flight) to allow the point of the next dart to slide down past it. Another is to link the shaft and the barrel with a spring so that the dart can bend if hit by another and so let it through. A third innovation is to allow the flight to rotate on the shaft to achieve the same effect. Adjustable shafts can be bought whose length can be altered to suit the player whilst ones made of new materials such as titanium or glass fibre are now available, though I cannot see what real advantages these possess over the more traditional types.

That this spate of new ideas has arisen in the last few years is naturally due to the corresponding rise in the game's popularity. Whether they catch on or not – for old ways die hard – they are all conceived to improve the standard of *your* game.

Your own set

There is no such thing as the perfect set of darts since everyone has their own preferences; this point is amply demonstrated by the widely different designs endorsed by the top players. The ultimate is to have your own personally designed set and several concerns prepared to produce such darts upon request advertise their services in the darts press. Alternatively many light engineering firms would be prepared to turn-up a set of barrels from a brass or tungsten alloy rod (again available through the trade papers). This service is of course an individual one and has to be paid for accordingly. Whilst such a set of arrows is of immense value in impressing your friends and neighbours, it is not a great deal of practical use unless your game is so good that this is the only way to improve it still further.

In any event, in designing your own darts you must be absolutely certain as to exactly what you want and this knowledge can only come through years of playing with a variety of darts; there is no short cut to finding the type of darts which best suit you. The main problem to solve is that of the weight. Players normally find that they get the greatest success with one particular weight of dart because it matches their personal throwing strength and style. A fast, strong 'push' action works best with heavy darts while a gentle, lobbing delivery requires a more delicate type. The most sensible way to discover what the ideal weight is for you is to borrow other people's darts whenever possible and experiment with them for a game or two, gradually narrowing down your preference. Then buy a set at that weight, play with them *a lot* – and only then consider making a final adjustment to a slightly heavier or lighter set. This process will naturally take time but it will be worth it. If you chop and change sets every month you will never get used to one weight and your game will suffer as a consequence.

The same system of trial and error can be carried out with regard to shafts and flights. Generally speaking, the longer the shaft the better balanced the dart will be as the weight increases. Find the optimum length for your own particular throwing action – one that doesn't poke your eye when you aim – and decide which of the various types of flight you are happiest with. Since modern darts are designed and manufactured to be capable of modification, don't be afraid to alter and adapt a factory-made set. Tom Barrett, one of the great names of the 1960s, even used to shave down his cane shafts to matchstick thickness to suit him better. With barrels available in about thirty weights in a variety of materials, shapes, lengths and grip patterns, with a good choice of shaft length and material and with a similar choice of flights, the resulting combination can be as tailor-made as an exclusively designed dart.

In common with most sports you only get what you pay for. Avoid sets that look and feel bulky and clumsy. Go for slimness and precision; choose as thin a barrel as possible for the weight you want. Providing they are well made, matched and balanced the rest is literally in your own hands. Practise with them, get used to their feel, and play, play, play. Only that way will you know whether or not they are right for you and, just as important, only that way, if they are not, will you know *why* not.

One other point to look for: Having found the weight and barrel design you like best, experiment if possible with different shaft/flight combinations and observe the results closely. A dart balanced for your own particular throw should stick in the board more or less horizontally; if the flight tends to point noticeably upwards, so obscuring part of the board, then change to either a smaller flight or a shorter shaft (or both). Similarly, if the dart tends to droop down from the board, correct with a larger area flight or a longer shaft (or both). Both of these defects can also be cured by changing to a longer or heavier barrel in the first case and to a shorter or lighter one in the second.

Care and maintenance

As with any other item of sports equipment, darts need to be looked after for the best results to be obtained. They should be protected when not in use, either by keeping them in the box in which they were sold or, in the case of ones with folding flights, in a plastic or leather wallet which can be bought for that purpose.

The only part of the dart which does not need specific attention is the barrel; everything else does. The point must be kept constantly sharpened – if in doubt, sharpen before a game. A dart that falls out is a dart wasted and possibly a game lost; the finer the point the better are the chances of it scraping round a wire rather than bouncing off it. The easiest way to keep one's set sharp is to invest a few pence in a special dart sharpener: a small cylinder or block of abrasive material with a hollow centre, similar to a pencil sharpener, inside which the dart's point is ground.

Shafts should be inspected regularly for damage, warping and looseness – all of which will affect a dart's performance. Push-fit canes are especially prone to coming adrift from their barrels; I wedge mine in with a slip of silver paper from a cigarette packet.

Flights should also be regularly examined for similar defects. They must be firmly attached to their shafts and with the slot-in variety it is advisable to check them continually during a game, preferably with an almost unconscious finger action before each one is thrown so that concentration is not broken. And if this seems over-cautious advice, count the number of darts that fall apart before reaching the board next time you are in a pub for an evening: you might be surprised. They should all be fitted exactly the same distance down their shafts and should be free from all nicks and kinks. The flight controls the path of the dart after it has left the hand; if you are doing your utmost to produce a perfect throw every time, imperfect flights simply mean that all your efforts are wasted. Small wonder that top players will fit a new set of flights before every match – and carry a spare with them.

However well you have looked after them, things will occasionally go wrong. If this does happen it is usually an easy matter to rectify the fault. One of the commonest mishaps is that the point falls out; the best way to secure it is with a smear of a suitable metal-to-metal glue such as Araldite. If for some reason a new point has to be fitted, this can be made by cutting a masonry fixing pin down to the required size and either gluing it in place or else, if the hole in the barrel is too narrow to take it, heat-shrinking it in. This is done by heating the barrel in a gas jet until it has expanded enough to take the new point; upon cooling the barrel will grip it securely. Damaged points can be removed in similar fashion: heat the barrel and pull out the point with a pair of pliers.

Damaged shafts should normally be straightaway replaced with ones of identical pattern. If however the split end of a nylon or plastic shaft has 'spread', this can be easily repaired. Simply bind the end with wire (or force it into an appropriate sized washer) and leave overnight in a cup of boiling water. The heat should be sufficient to remould the shaft to its original shape. Cane shafts overcome this problem to some extent by virtue of the metal clip supplied with them that grips the cane just below the flight. As bought, the canes are not split and a + shaped cut has to be made in one end with a sharp blade. The wide end also presents a major obstacle to other darts and after cutting it is worthwhile sanding down the split section to a gentle taper (*see* Fig 11).

Plastic folding flights are prone to splitting after repeated contact with other darts and are simply best replaced. The same holds true for the paper variety. Feather flights, on the other hand, are more expensive and are worth looking after. A useful tip here is to run a spot of clear varnish or glue (nail varnish is ideal) down the shaft between the feathers to give them added strength and resilience; slightly damaged sections can also be touched-up with the same fluid. A drop on the tips is a good idea if a metal protector is not fitted.

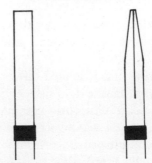

Fig 11 Cane shaft (left) as bought and (right) as split and tapered

In short, keep your darts in the best condition at all times and the results should fully justify the negligible expense involved.

Nails

If you really want to impress your friends, obtain a set of nails. Real nails. I cannot claim to know exactly when nail-throwing was first introduced into the world of darts but it must have been a good few years ago. Several of the great names in darts history have included the feat in their exhibition repetoire and the greatest of them all is generally reckoned to have been Joe Hitchcock. Any type of nail can be used but those normally chosen are 4–6in in length, because of their weight, and ground to a fine point. Masonry nails are the best for durability.

That is all there is to it. That and practice, practice and yet more practice. Since they are inherently unstable in flight they are not thrown like a normal dart but like a knife, completing a number of turns (or half-turns depending on whether they are thrown point- or head-first) before plunging into the board. The best style is that which suits you and has to be worked out by hours of effort before the action is perfected. Then you can go onto the stunts and trick shots such as knocking cigarettes out of someone's mouth and pinning them to the board, coins off spectacles, pills off tongues. Or good old 301 of course. I wouldn't know but it must be a good feeling to beat someone in a normal game using a set of nails.

5 Improving your game

It might well be regarded as presumptious of me to write such a chapter, being merely a poor pub player with no trophies or titles to my name. Since I am however a firm believer in Dr Johnson's dictum that you do not have to be a master carpenter to know whether a table rocks or not, I have attempted to set out some of the more basic points of the game which ought to be remembered, noted or mastered so that any player might produce his or her best level of performance.

Far more expert advice has been kindly supplied by the England international player Tony Brown and I have added in his comments where appropriate. His tips are derived from experience at the very highest levels of the game – and from a whole string of successes in both the national and international scene. Tony:

> Some people say that good darts players are born and not made. This may be true to a certain extent but a novice may reach an acceptable standard by adopting the right stance, using the right equipment and practising regularly.

The essentials

PRACTICE

The most fundamental of all the basics is practice. No one ever became proficient at darts by sitting behind a pint pot watching others play. If top professionals feel the need to practice several hours a day whenever possible, then us lesser mortals need to spend all the time on the board we can. Going round on doubles and trebles is as good a way as any – but more important still are actual games against someone else, preferably of a slightly higher standard to bring out your best. Tony:

Some of the best ways of practising when you are on your own are to go round the board in doubles; throw at two- and three-dart finishes and to have ten throws at treble twenty, working our your average score. By doing this you can measure your improvement in consistency. Also, try and throw with a toe-bar up whenever possible to get used to competition conditions.

EQUIPMENT
There are people who can throw mis-matched darts with half their flights missing (an ordinary set of 'pub's own' darts in other words!) better than I can my own – but then there are also those who can throw six-inch nails and score a ton a time. For normal players though, their game can only be as good as their darts – and by good I do not necessarily mean expensive. As already stated in Chapter 4, they should be well matched to each other, well balanced in flight and well suited to the thrower; they should also be kept perfectly sharp, perfectly flighted and generally properly looked after. If a dart fails to land where it was aimed then the fault should lie with the thrower, not the dart, so that it can at least be partly remedied through practice. If a dart does not fly true then no amount of practice will ever make it do so.

Also remember when buying a set that it is no use having room for just one dart in the treble twenty bed: all three *must* be able to fit into that half of a square inch. You might not be able to achieve such a feat today – but tomorrow, who knows? When the chance comes you can be confident that it is within the capabilities of your arrows, if not yourself. Tony:

The average weight of darts used by players today is about 24g although this is arrived at by weights ranging from 15g to 40g. Lighter darts tend to be affected more easily by draughts than heavier ones and whereas a light dart will rebound from a wire, a heavier dart might glance off and stick in the board due to the extra weight behind it. I personally use 18g darts.

Once a player has selected a set of darts that suit him he must stick with them and give them a fair trial. Sometimes, because they have a bad game with a particular set, players discard them and look for another type of dart, forgetting that yesterday they played well with them. So persevere and give yourself time to get used to the darts you have selected.

Generally speaking, a good darts player can throw most sets of darts reasonably well but it does not mean, necessarily, that an expensive set of darts will transform an average player into a really good one.

I know tungsten darts are expensive but once you have decided on the set of darts for you try and get another set exactly the same so that you have replacements on the spot in case of mishaps such as points snapping.

Carry your own sharpener.

THE THROW

There are innumerable ways of throwing a dart at the board. I have encountered good underarm players and some people, for a change, like to throw their arrows flight-first so they turn end over end, like a knife, before hitting the board. On the whole though the normal, overarm launch from in front of the face is generally thought the best. It is all a simple question of sighting. To give a parallel example: never mind what they do in westerns, the way to fire a pistol accurately is to sight along the barrel, not blast away wildly from the hip. The same is true of darts: with a delivery begun either just below or just beside the appropriate eye both target and dart are in the same line of vision when the one is released at the other. Tony:

The ideal throwing style is to use mainly the wrist and not the arm (as when throwing a javelin) and to try and throw every dart with the same action, although sometimes due to tension and trying too hard a player may alter his action by 'snatching', thus impairing his true aim.

THE STANCE

There are two main schools of thought about the stance that should be adopted for the throw. The first advocates a sideways-on position with the right foot (for righthanded throwers) pointing at the board from the hockey and the left foot behind and at more or less right-angles to its mate. Thus the whole body leans towards the board during delivery so that at the actual moment of release the right hand, swinging forwards from the elbow, is as near to the board as could be possible while the weight of the body is supported by the braced front foot. The second school of thought favours a chest-on stance with the feet firmly planted apart, both toeing the hockey. During delivery the body remains upright so as to provide a solid support for the leverage of the throwing arm. The best advice I can give, having tried both positions myself, is to adopt the one that feels the most natural and the most comfortable. All that really matters is that the stance should be *stable;* if you wobble about whilst throwing (no one-legged imitations of Eros please) don't be surprised if your darts follow suit!

Still on the subject of the stance, there is one other point to be considered. Some players will remain on the same spot for their three darts, apparently rooted to the floor, while others, if you watch them closely, will shift from side to side behind the hockey according to where the next dart has to go. There are two reasons for this. One is that it makes sense to always throw from exactly opposite the bed aimed at since, by doing so, you are standardising your throw as much as possible, thus making it easier to control. The second reason is that the first dart might be blocking an important double or treble bed from where you are standing and you have to alter position to get a clear shot at it. A gentler, lobbing action should carry a dart in over another obscuring a bed whilst gripping a dart slightly further back than usual and throwing it slightly harder than usual should push a dart in directly underneath another. Again, do whatever comes naturally to you — but above all be consistent. Hopping to and fro behind the hockey is not likely to aid concentration — though in my favourite pub no one moves across the hockey since there is simply no room to after about eight o'clock and strangers can be seen to flinch as darts soar head-high beside the bar only inches from them. Tony:

> The main point about stance or style is that a player *must* feel comfortable while he is throwing. Top players may be involved in exhibitions or tournaments that last for anything up to five hours so it is very important that they have the stance to enable them to do this without getting cramp or feeling uncomfortable.

STATE OF MIND
Tony:

Darts is very much a game of the mind depending very often on how you feel. Your mind must be free from worry for you to apply yourself to give your best and even a row with the wife or girlfriend before you go to the match may upset you. It is important, especially for a professional, that your partner is interested in the game and willing that you participate in it.

To be reasonably fit can be an advantage because a tournament may go on all day and will end up a test of stamina as well as skill.

Most players prefer a few pints before they play which tends to relax them and enables them to absorb the atmosphere of the occasion, although this again is up to the individual.

When playing a top player forget who he is; remember – you have three darts in your hand the same as your opponent.

The best way to improve your game is to keep playing top opposition and even though you may be well beaten at first, after a while your improvement will be seen as you give him a harder game. I use a term, "you have got to lose before you win". Nobody starts off winning all the time and when you play top class opposition you must expect to lose as many as you win. To accept losing is the main point and, after congratulating your opponent, look forward to your next game.

DRESS
Finally, a note on dress. Anything within the recognised bounds of decency goes but bear in mind that the top players do not play in short, loose sleeves for nothing. Just as table-tennis players discovered the value of unrestricting clothing, so have darts players. The throwing arm should be free to move unhindered by tight jackets or shirtsleeves. It must however be admitted that in some circumstances a touch of gamesmanship can be more than effective: I was always at my worst against a certain league player after he had nonchalantly hit a ton on his warm-up throw without bothering to remove his winter's coat.

Preferences

Preferences play an important role in darts: this double, that double; this side of the board, that side. Everyone has them and the more I have observed them, the more sure I am that such preferences are purely psychological. I have seen left-handed players prefer the same areas of the board as right-handed players and totally different areas preferred by otherwise identical throwers. Even more interesting is the fact that preferences are easily switched across the board – sometimes after years, sometimes after weeks. My own favourite double at any one time is 6, 10, 5, 14 or 20. Usually! What seems to happen is that a player will start or finish a game with ease on one particular double, repeat the feat and so become inordinately fond of it – until in turn it is usurped by some other.

The commonest preferences are the easiest or most useful ones: the left or right side of the board for starting – the near-vertical alignment of the doubles here presents an easier target for most throwing actions – 20x or 16x for finishing and 20t or 19t for scoring. Although it means that the other numbers tend to be neglected by comparison, this is more than compensated for by the confidence inspired by the results obtained from old favourites.

A friend of mine came back from a holiday in the Channel Islands with the following tale which illustrates the point well. He had been playing one day in a pub and had become stuck trying to hit double five for game shot. His opponent was similarly helpless, whereupon the landlord said 'You need old Arthur to get that for you'.

To much encouragement and cries of 'Do your stuff, Arthur' and 'You show 'em, Arthur' etc, an ancient, white-haired gentleman shuffled up to the hockey, selected a dart, hurled it unerringly into the very centre of the double five bed and returned to his seat amidst all-round applause.

'Never misses double five', confided the publican. 'Never throws for anything else, mind. Hasn't for the last seventeen years.'

6 The mathematics of the game

The importance of mental arithmetic in darts cannot be overestimated. Indeed, it could be said that it is as vital a part of the game as any other. As well as knowing what he is throwing for, a good player will know after each dart where the next one should be aimed – and what to switch to if he misses. Pausing to work out what score is left in the middle of a throw not only wastes time but also breaks the concentration and rhythm so necessary for consistent play. This chapter sets out to explain just what is involved in this side of the game and gives a number of short-cuts to acquiring this ability. The calculations needed are not difficult ones and the commonest can be picked up quite simply by repetition as they frequently recur in games. Tony Brown puts the professional viewpoint:

> Counting ability is very important at top level where, if you give your opponent one dart at a double, you must expect to lose. I would say that learning to count and knowing your shots is more than half the battle to become a good darts player. It is, perhaps, the equivalent of putting the white ball where you want it in snooker.

To begin with, the most fundamental step is to learn the position of each number on the board; this should take even the rawest novice a handful of games at the most. After that the values of all the doubles and trebles have to be learnt; again, this will take but little study and play. (As with everything else in this chapter, the more frequent the play the easier will be the whole learning process.) Then comes the memorizing of all the possible multiples of a given number (*see* Fig 12); next, what to go for if a certain double is split (*see* Fig 14).

The last stage can only come with time and practice but it is well worth the effort to try and master at least part of it. As they arise various combinations of numbers should be recognised for what they add up to: 59 left is 19 and 20x, 11 left is 3 and 4x and so on. Since the number of possible permutations is astronomical, there is no value in even attempting to tabulate them all. However a useful tip when on a high number is to take either 40 (20x) or 32 (16x) from the score and then split the remainder, thereby leaving that double (20x or 16x) as the last dart. A recommended list of possible 3-dart game shots is given in Fig 13 and a 2-dart list in Fig 15. These are generally recognised as the best finishes, although they do not all end with 20x or 16x, since they are the easiest alternatives, leave a good double to end on, require as little moving round the board as possible – and will give you at least a fair score if you miss!

Fig 12 Possible scores with three darts on one number

No.	x2	x3	x4	x5	x6	x7	x8	x9
1	2	3	4	5	6	7	8	9
2	4	6	8	10	12	14	16	18
3	6	9	12	15	18	21	24	27
4	8	12	16	20	24	28	32	36
5	10	15	20	25	30	35	40	45
6	12	18	24	30	36	42	48	54
7	14	21	28	35	42	49	56	63
8	16	24	32	40	48	56	64	72
9	18	27	36	45	54	63	72	81
10	20	30	40	50	60	70	80	90
11	22	33	44	55	66	77	88	99
12	24	36	48	60	72	84	96	108
13	26	39	52	65	78	91	104	117
14	28	42	56	70	84	98	112	126
15	30	45	60	75	90	105	120	135
16	32	48	64	80	96	112	128	144
17	34	51	68	85	102	119	136	153
18	36	54	72	90	108	126	144	162
19	38	57	76	95	114	133	152	171
20	40	60	80	100	120	140	160	180
25	50	75	100	125	150	—	—	—

Note: x3 equals three singles, one treble, a single plus a double; x6 equals two trebles, shanghai or three doubles, and so on.

Fig 13 Game shots with three darts

170 20t-20t-50	139 19t-14t-20x	114 20t-18-18x
	138 20t-18t-12x	113 19t-16-20x
167 19t-20t-50	137 19t-16t-16x	112 20t-20-16x
164 20t-18t-50	136 20t-20t-8x	111 17t-20-20x
161 17t-20t-50	135 20t-15t-15x	110 20t-18-16x
160 20t-20t-20x	134 20t-14t-16x	
	133 20t-19t-8x	109 19t-20-16x
158 20t-20t-19x	132 20t-16t-12x	108 20t-16-16x
157 19t-20t-20x	131 20t-13t-16x	107 19t-18-16x
156 20t-20t-18x	130 20t-18t-8x	106 20t-14-16x
155 20t-19t-19x		105 15t-20-20x
154 18t-20t-20x	129 19t-16t-12x	104 19t-16-16x
153 20t-19t-18x	128 20t-20t-4x	103 17t-20-16x
152 20t-20t-16x	127 20t-17t-8x	102 20t-10-16x
151 17t-20t-20x	126 20t-15x-18x	101 17t-18-16x
150 20t-18t-18x	125 20t-25-20x	
	124 20t-16t-8x	99 19t-10-16x
149 19t-20t-16x	123 19t-14t-12x	
148 16t-20t-20x	122 20t-15x-16x	*100 and all numbers*
147 20t-17t-18x	121 17t-10t-20x	*from 98 down to 41*
146 20t-18t-16x	120 20t-20-20x	*can be scored in two*
145 15t-20t-20x		*darts*
144 20t-20t-12x	119 19t-10-16x	
143 20t-17t-16x	118 20t-18-20x	
142 14t-20t-20x	117 19t-20-20x	
141 20t-15t-18x	116 20t-20-18x	
140 20t-16t-16x	115 19t-18-20x	

Fig 14 Best shots after splitting a double with first dart

Double split	Best throw with remaining darts
20x	10x
19x	3–8x
18x	9x
17x	1–8x
16x	8x
15x	7–4x
14x	7x, 6–4x, 10–2x according to preference
13x	5–4x
12x	6x
11x	3–4x
10x	5x, 2–4x, 6–2x according to preference
9x	1–4x
8x	4x
7x	3–2x
6x	3x, 2–2x according to preference
5x	1–2x
4x	2x

Below 4 there is no choice of throws.

Fig 15 Game shots with two darts

110	20t-50	82	14t-20x	59	19-20x
		81	15t-18x	58	18-20x
107	19t-50	80	16t-16x	57	17-20x
104	18t-50			56	16-20x
101	17-50	79	17t-14x	55	15-20x
100	20t-20x	78	18t-12x	54	18-18x or 14-20x
		77	19t-10x	53	13-20x
98	20t-19x	76	20t-18x	52	20-16x or 12-20x
97	19t-20x	75	15t-15x	51	19-16x or 11-20x
96	20t-18x	74	14t-16x	50	18-16x or 10-20x
95	19t-19x	73	19t-8x		
94	18t-20x	72	16t-12x	49	17-16x or 9-20x
93	19t-18x	71	13t-16x	48	16-16x or 8-20x
92	20t-16x	70	15x-20x	47	15-16x or 7-20x
91	17t-20x			46	14-16x or 6-20x
90	18t-18x	69	19t-6x	45	13-16x or 5-20x
		68	20t-4x	44	12-16x or 4-20x
89	19t-16x	67	17t-8x	43	11-16x or 3-20x
88	16t-20x	66	15x-18x	42	10-16x or 2-20x
87	17t-18x	65	25-20x	41	9-16x or 1-20x
86	18t-16x	64	16t-8x		
85	15t-20x	63	17t-6x		*50 and all even numbers below*
84	20t-12x	62	15x-16x		*41 can be scored with one dart;*
83	17t-16x	61	25-18x		*odd numbers below 40 (except 1)*
		60	20-20x		*require two eg 39=7-16x*

Tony:

> Most important is the ability to be able to keep throwing when your first dart has missed the target. Your mind must work out what is required and your second dart must be on the way without hesitation or break of concentration.

Do not let any of these tables put you off. I know people who can add two and two together on paper and make five yet can perform quite prodigious feats of mental arithmetic when placed in front of a dartboard. (A similar phenomenon can be observed amongst crib players.)

Since the primary object of the game is to reduce the total and be out as quickly as possible, game shots should always be attempted however remote you think are your chances of getting them. For example, if left with 73 you can either play safe and get, say, 20-10-3 to leave you 20x for your next throw or you can go for 11t-20x or 19t-8x to give you game shot that throw. Your opponent is not going to hang about waiting for you to finish and if you shirk the hard ones you will never get the competitive practice, and the confidence, needed to hit them.

Some basic facts

Every player should know certain basic facts about the arithmetic of the game which are part of its very structure. Listed below, these should be learnt not in isolation but rather for their value in planning throws. For example, any score over 170 *cannot* be a possible game shot and so a player ought to be automatically calculating the best way to bring his total below this figure and at the same time leave himself the chance of an easy game shot for his next throw. Similarly, he will be able the better to assess his own position in the game with regard to his opponent's.

The standard game
Highest score possible: 180 (20t-20t-20t)
Highest score possible with two darts: 120 (20t-20t)

Highest score possible with one dart: 60 (20t)
Highest shot out: 170 (20t-20t-50)
Highest shot out with two darts: 110 (20t-50)
Highest shot out with one dart: 50
Lowest score not possible: 163
Lowest score not possible with two darts: 103
Lowest score not possible with one dart: 23
Lowest even number not possible as game shot: 162
Lowest shot out not possible: 159
Lowest shot out not possible with two darts: 99
Longest (safest) run of split doubles: 16x-8x-4x-2x-1x

101
Shortest possible game (double start); three darts (20x-19t-2x)

201
Shortest possible game (double start): four darts (20x-20t-17t, 50)

301
Shortest possible game (double or straight start): six darts (20x-20t-20t, 20t-17t-15x)

401
Shortest possible game (straight start): seven darts (20t-20t-20t, 20t-20t-17, 50)
Shortest possible game (double start): eight darts (20x-20t-20t, 20t-20t-20t, 7t-20x)

501
Shortest possible game (double or straight start): nine darts (50-20t-20t, 20t-20t-20t, 20t-17t-20x)

601
Shortest possible game (straight off): eleven darts (20t-20t-20t, 20t-20t-20t, 20t-20t-20t, 7t-20x)

701
Shortest possible game (straight off): twelve darts (20t-20t-20t, 20t-20t-20t, 20t-20t-20t, 20t-17t-50)

801
Shortest possible game (straight off): fourteen darts (20t-20t-20t, 20t-20t-20t, 20t-20t-20t, 20t-20t-20t, 17t-15x)

901
Shortest possible game (straight off): sixteen darts (20t-20t-20t, 20t-20t-20t, 20t-20t-20t, 20t-20t-20t, 20t-20t-7t, 20x)

1,001
Shortest possible game (straight off): seventeen darts (20t-20t-20t, 20t-20t-20t, 20t-20t-20t, 20t-20t-20t, 20t-20t-20t, 17t-50) Only one player has apparently ever achieved this near-impossible feat: Alan Glazier of England in 1977.

7 Getting to the top

The bad news is that, unless you are a one-in-a-million natural genius at the game, there is no short-cut to the top in the darts world. The good news is that virtually anyone can make at least part of that journey providing they are prepared to put a great deal of time and effort into the game.

Dedication

The most important requirement needed for a budding professional player (or a top-class amateur) is undoubtedly an unswerving dedication to the game. This is certainly the main difference between the 'friendly' and the 'serious' player. The 'friendly' player is someone who is content to play at his local in the evening and perhaps play for their team once a week; the 'serious' player is someone who sees this level of the game as just the first step on the ladder to greater things such as county and national team membership. In practical terms it means being prepared to play any time, anywhere, and accepting that this might involve time off work, travelling expenses, etc. So you cannot afford to be half-hearted in your attempt to get to the top: the enthusiasm and dedication must be both total and constant.

Perfection

The second vital requirement needed to make it to the top is being prepared to struggle continually to perfect your game. Regular practice is essential, both at home on specific targets such as doubles, and in match and competition play. The latter will build up vital experience since no professional player can allow his nerves to fail when the pressure is on.

Fitness

Today's top players will stress the importance of physical fitness in the modern game. Major tournaments can and do go on for several hours at a stretch and the more rounds you win, the greater the sheer strain of maintaining the same balanced stance and throwing action. Keep fit, exercise regularly and make sure your stance and action can stand up to the sort of strain that you hope you will have to face.

Drink always has been and should be a necessary part of the atmosphere of darts. World-class players will naturally consume different amounts of drink during a match, ranging from none at all up to several pints and there can be no hard and fast rule. But most of these players would agree that a moderate amount of drink seems to have a beneficial action in relaxing the body slightly and easing the tension of the occasion. The secret is to discover just what a 'moderate amount' is for you – and then stick to that limit.

Just as vital as physical fitness is mental fitness: you must be able to put out of your mind all personal worries and problems during every game, leaving yourself free to concentrate exclusively on the matter in hand.

The road to the top

If you can honestly say that you satisfy *all* the above requirements then you are well on the way to success; the higher you climb though, the more you will discover that everyone else is equally prepared and dedicated and the real test of skill and ability then begins in earnest.

To start at the bottom of the competitive ladder, find out the league structure in you own locality (from the local sports press) and become a regular player (if you are not one already) at a pub that fields a team. Sooner or later, if you are good enough, you will make the team. (This is probably easier to do if the pub or club boasts more than one team.) After that comes selection for the super league and county side and then the ultimate, the national squad.

There is a parallel route to the top which should also be taken at the same time as that through match play. This is via the growing number of local and national tournaments. Many of these (certainly the more local or regional ones) are open to all upon payment of an entry fee and they encompass pairs and team competitions as well as singles; be prepared to spend time and money in entering as many as you can. Some are only open to members of the various darts organisations so join those for which you are eligible (certainly the national ones for which see the *Appendices*). Keep track of what is going on and where by subscribing to the darts press (see the *Bibliography*); if you are dedicated, talented and take the opportunities, then the titles and prizes will come. If you do not have what it takes then at least you will have found out for sure. If you have, then the professional path of financial sponsorship, product endorsement and the big-money circuit lies temptingly ahead.

Part III:
Other boards, other games

8 Other boards

The London board is by no means the only dartboard in use in this country. In the same way that there are traditional strongholds of different patterned dominoes, so there are several other regional designs of board still in regular use throughout the British Isles. Each has its own degree of peculiarity which links it firmly to its own particular locality. Long may they continue to be used, and it seems likely that in view of the growing interest in darts they will not be allowed to die out (despite strong pressure from certain quarters to standardize the game) if only for the practical reason that many of them can be produced by means of minor modifications to the London board either during or after manufacture. In the final analysis, darts is a pub game and what the regulars say is what goes!

EAST END BOARD
Undoubtedly the oddest of all regional boards is the one almost solely confined to the East End of London with other small pockets of use in the neighbouring parts of Suffolk, Essex and Kent, probably due to a large-scale migration of East Enders at some time or other to these places. It is also known as the Fives board on account of its unique numbering system. (*See* Fig 16.)

It is tempting to suppose that this board represents a primitive stage in the evolution of the dartboard; indeed the low number of actual segments (twelve) and the simple numbering system used (20, 5, 15, 10, 20, 5, 15, 10, 20, 5, 15, 10) lend weight to this theory. The fact that the board also incorporates an outer bull

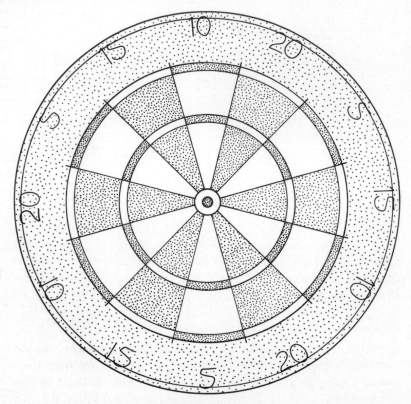

Fig 16 The East End board

and a trebles ring lends weight in turn to the idea that these are
southern innovations – the northern designs described below
lack at least one of these beds. The diameter of the scoring area is
slightly less than that of the London board (by an inch or so)
with correspondingly narrower doubles and trebles ($\frac{1}{4}$in); in the
East End itself the doubles and trebles are only half this width!

MANCHESTER BOARD
This pattern of board is also known as the Lancashire or log-end
board – the latter name harking back to its probable origins. In
appearance (indeed, like all the segmented boards) it closely
resembles the end of a sawn-off log with the doubles ring
representing the bark, the bull the central core, and the segments
the wood between the cracks radiating from it. (*See* Fig 17.)

The various beds of this board comprise the numbers 1 to 20, their narrow ($\frac{1}{8}$in) doubles and the 25 and 50 bulls. There are no trebles. Another special feature is that the numbers are set out differently from the London board (clockwise from the top): 4, 20, 1, 16, 6, 17, 8, 12, 9, 14, 5, 19, 2, 15, 3, 18, 7, 11, 10 and 13. The playing area is also far smaller than both the London and East End boards – at 10in the size of an ordinary dinner plate! All in all it is certainly the most difficult board on which to play and anyone electing to do so is justifiably proud of that fact. As

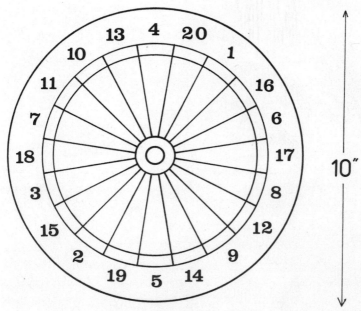

Fig 17 The Manchester board

the name implies its stronghold is Manchester and the surrounding area and any attempt to displace it in favour of the London board is fiercely resisted.

The log-end theory is supported by the fact that by tradition it is more commonly made of elm than other boards (though cork is sometimes now used). Between sessions it is kept soaked in water or beer slops in order to maintain its receptiveness; sometimes two boards are used, one in play and one for soaking. If left to dry out the 'wires', which are actually metal strips embedded in the wood, tend to spring out and the whole board will start to crack and split.

YORKSHIRE BOARD
Coming nearer to the London board in design is the Yorkshire board with its distinctive differences to its rival across the Pennines. (*See* Fig 18.) Although it lacks trebles and the 25 bull,

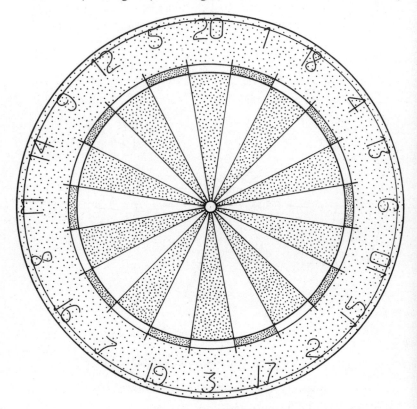

Fig 18 The Yorkshire board

it uses the London pattern of numbering and is the same size as the southern board. Traditionally the doubles ring is also narrow ($\frac{1}{4}$in) but since this pattern of board is often manufactured by omitting certain wires from the spider of a London board the wide double ring can sometimes be found.

It is used mainly in the Yorkshire region but can also be met with in parts of Staffordshire and the North Midlands.

KENT BOARD
A board identical to the Yorkshire pattern, traditionally used in parts of Kent and known there by that name.

Fig 19 The Tonbridge board

LINCOLN BOARD
Again similar to the Yorkshire board; as used in the Lincolnshire area this board is traditionally uniformly coloured black.

IRISH BOARD
A third board based on the Yorkshire style is that used in Ireland. Like the Lincoln board it too is traditionally all-black.

Taken together, the Yorkshire, Kent, Lincoln and Irish

boards make this design the most widely used by far after the London board.

TONBRIDGE BOARD

The first of a distinctly unusual trio of boards. Used in the Tonbridge-Sevenoaks area of Kent, this board's other name of the Trebles board denotes its special peculiarity: what would be the *doubles* ring on a London board is used as the *trebles* ring. The numbering of the segments and general dimensions are the same as the London board but there is no outer bull and no 'conventional' trebles ring. The doubles on this board consist of triangular beds inside the trebles (*see* Fig 19) which calls for some fine throwing indeed!

Fig 20 The Staffordshire board

STAFFORDSHIRE BOARD

Also known as the Burton board, the second board of this trio is unique in that it has two beds *outside* the normal scoring area. (*See* Fig 20.) Otherwise it resembles the Yorkshire board but with an outer bull. The two extra beds are 1in square diamonds set midway between the 14 and 9 segments on the left and the 4 and 13 segments on the right in the non-scoring surround. They are each worth 25 and can also be used as a shot out on that number at the end of a game of 301.

This board as normally used is of wooden construction but at one time it was traditionally produced in clay from the local potteries.

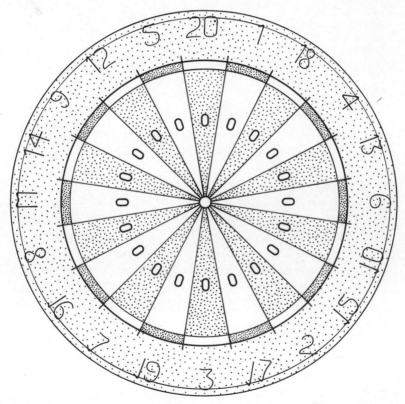

Fig 21 The Club board

CLUB BOARD

Also known as the tournament board, this last board of the segmented type has unique oval treble beds and no outer bull. (*See* Fig 21.) Otherwise it is similar to the London board. Its stronghold was at one time workingmen's clubs rather than a specific town or region – and according to local rules the bull apparently scored either 50 or 100. It is now believed to be extinct.

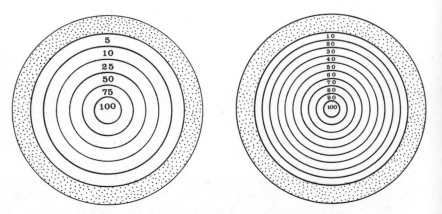

Fig 22 The two patterns of target-faced board

TARGET BOARD

As far as I am aware, this board is not used at all in Britain – again I have never seen one – though some reference books suggest that it is still used in the USA and possibly elsewhere. As its name suggests, it has an archery target type face composed of concentric rings around a bull. At least two different designs have been recorded: the first is for a 100 bull and five rings scoring (outwards) 75, 50, 25, 10 and 5; the second is for a 100 bull again and nine rings scoring (outwards) 90, 80, 70, 60, 50, 40, 30, 20 and 10. (*See* Fig 22.)

For reasons that will be examined in Chapter 10, this pattern of board is markedly inferior to the segmented variety and its use has never caught on in Britain.

Early boards

Besides those boards described above, there are at least three other designs recorded but now certainly out of use. These are, for want of better names, the Norfolk, Grimsby and Gloucester boards. The first two of the three are especially important in helping to fill out the whole history of the dartboard.

NORFOLK BOARD
Described by Arthur Taylor in his book *Pub Games* (1976), this was apparently in use in parts of Norfolk up to the 1940s. It was made of elm and obviously drew its inspiration directly from an archery target. (*See* Fig 23.) Circular and about 10in across, it

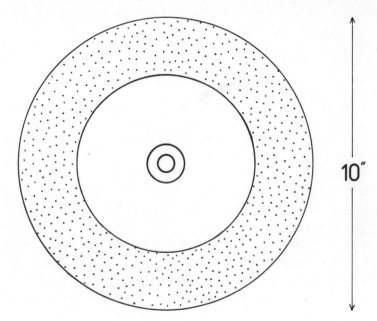

Fig 23 The Norfolk board

comprised a bull of about 1in, a 2in diameter outer bull and a third scoring ring about 6in across. Score values were: inner bull 4, outer bull 3, third ring 1. On this simple board an equally simple game was played: plain scoring up to 31, pegged on a cribbage board.

GRIMSBY BOARD

In use at the turn of the century in Grimsby, this board was similar to the neighbouring Yorkshire pattern but contained no less than twenty-eight segments! Since it called for its own peculiar brand of mental arithmetic it is highly likely that the locals could find no one else willing to play them on it, hence its abandonment!

GLOUCESTER BOARD

Modelled on a London board, this was no less than twice the normal size with correspondingly widened doubles and trebles. According to Croft-Cooke it was manufactured in Cirencester (as a novelty?) and was no easier to play on than an ordinary board – seems very hard to believe!

A possible evolution

It is impossible to be dogmatic about the evolution of dartboard design or the proliferation of regional variations; what is possible though is to examine what evidence we have and attempt to trace its development.

The development and design of the archery target will be dealt with in Chapter 10, together with the various theories about the origins of the game of darts; suffice it to say here that it is highly probable that the very first boards were of the target variety but these quickly gave way to the segmented pattern. The Norfolk board was surely the last remaining leftover from those early days; indeed, one could hardly invent a simpler (or more boring) board. The idea of segments then spread throughout the country, though naturally the process could not have been uniform in time or manner. If an actual board was moved then a new region had a pattern to copy; if however only the *description* of a board was passed on by a traveller, then such details as the number of segments and their numbering would be liable to alteration in the telling. Apparently unchanged though was the basic principle of the board and the recognised fact that high numbers should be placed next to low ones wherever possible.

BOARD	FEATURES							
	Bull	Segments	Doubles	1-20	London order	Two colours	Trebles	Doubles and trebles rings
Norfolk	*							
Grimsby	*	*	*					
Manchester	*	*	*	*				
Irish / Lincoln	*	*	*	*	*			
Yorks / Kent	*	*	*	*	*	*		
Staffs	*	*	*	*	*	*		
Club	*	*	*	*	*	*	*	
Tonbridge	*	*	*	*	*	*	*	
East End	*	*	*			*	*	*
London	*	*	*	*	*	*	*	*

Fig 24

Fig 24 attempts to impose some sort of order on the evidence afforded by the different recorded boards. The various identifying factors of the London board are set out from left to right and the regional boards are ranked vertically according to the number of features possessed. Thus all boards feature a bull, all but the Norfolk feature segments, all but the Norfolk, Grimsby and East End boards feature twenty segments, etc.

It is tempting to equate the vertical ranking of the different boards in Fig 24 with an age order, especially as it seems likely that the more sophisticated the board, the more modern it is. Thus the idea of doubles is older and more widespread than that of trebles; a two-colour board is a later development of an all-black board.

Another interesting suggestion is that the treble ring must almost certainly be a London invention as it appears only on the London and East End boards (with an intriguing variation on the neighbouring Tonbridge board).

How then did the present London board evolve? My own theory is that the earliest segmented boards, which replaced the target boards, consisted of a random number of segments radiating from a central bull. The bull itself was retained from the target boards and appeared as a single or inner and outer bull according to local preference. On a purely practical level, simply by virtue of the fact that all the segment wires cannot meet at a single point, a bull *has* to be produced. The next major innovation on the board after the introduction of segments was the doubles ring. Its purpose was ingenious in that it could produce high scores but created the risk of scoring nothing. In this it was a logical progression from the idea of segments with high numbers next to low ones.

The actual number of segments varied from as few as twelve on the East End board to the twenty-eight of the Grimsby.board. These are probably close to the extremes beyond which the game would become spoilt through being too easy, too difficult or too dependent upon luck. Twenty was settled on in most places simply because it was a round number and split the board up neatly. Doubtless there were variations on the numbering system that have long since vanished but eventually just two won out: the Yorkshire and the Manchester patterns (ignoring the special case of the East End board).

By the turn of the century the basic board was black with doubles and (apart from the Manchester idiosyncrasy) numbered in the London order – a black Yorkshire board which must have been in use up and down the country (see the Thurston quote's description at the very beginning of this book). No doubt Yorkshiremen have been saying it for years but their board has a far better claim to being Britain's 'standard' dartboard than the London one! Be that as it may, after some odd experiments with the idea of trebles (again, a logical development) in the Club and Tonbridge boards, the London board adopted the pattern of the present trebles ring, as did its neighbour the East End board. From then on, as with much else originating in the capital, the treble-ringed board gradually spread out through the country, taking with it its two-tone colour scheme. Aided by the growing degree of organisation and standardisation in the wake of national tournaments (of which the first, the *News of the World* competition, likewise began in London) the London board was adopted as the 'standard'. New ideas may come and go, such as the diamonds on the Staffordshire board, but they are not likely to fundamentally alter the balanced design of the London board.

9 Other games

In addition to the standard game and its variants there are many other games which are regularly played on dartboards up and down the country. Although played only for amusement or a small stake, each in its own way provides valuable practice for the different throws needed in the standard game. Several of the more popular and widespread of these games are described below; all can be played by just two players though some are far better suited to larger numbers, either as a team contest or in a grand free-for-all.

Three general points regarding these games should be noted. Firstly, where players start the game with a number of 'lives' (usually three or five, depending on the time factor), these are marked as vertical chalk strokes beside each players' initial(s) on the scoreboard and erased when lost. Secondly, players usually throw for the bull to determine order of play but when large numbers are involved it is often easier to throw in straightforward alphabetical order. Lastly, unless otherwise stated, each player's throw consists of three darts in the normal manner.

After each game I have added a note on what I judge to be the best tactics for playing it; some of the games are however so straightforward that no special tactics are called for, just the ability to hit the target accurately!

Games for two players

Some of these games may also be played by two pairs in which case partners can be picked by throwing for the bull: nearest and furthest play together against the other two, combining their scores as when playing the standard game.

77

ALL FIVES

Each player aims to score a multiple of 5 for his total throw (eg 15, 45 and so on). All three darts *must* score something otherwise the throw is discounted. The number of 5s scored is then totalled (eg 15 counts as 3, 45 as 9 and so on). The first player to reach 51 points wins the game.

A common variation is that the winning score of 51 must be reached exactly so if a player has 50 points then his winning throw must score just 5. If he scores anything else then the throw is discounted.

Tactics: Concentrate on the 5-20 quadrant of the board. Landing all three darts within these two numbers will ensure a score every throw. Aim for the treble beds for maximum points.

GOLF

Like several of the games in this chapter, this one takes its inspiration from another sport. The basics are simple: the numbers 1-18 on the dartboard represent the eighteen holes of a golf course and each player must score three of each number in turn before progressing to the next 'hole'. Scoring is by the number of 'strokes' taken at each hole – a treble counts as a hole in 1, a double and a single counts as 2, three misses and three singles count 6 and so on. A player stays on the board until he gets his three on that number regardless of how many darts it takes him. Lowest total score at the end of the 'round' wins the game. (*See* Fig 25.)

A		B	A		B
1	1	2	22	10	33
3	2	6	24	11	39
7	3	9	28	12	42
8	4	14	30	13	
11	5	20		14	
13	6	23		15	
16	7	26		16	
18	8	30		17	
21	9	31		18	

Fig 25 Typical Golf scoreboard; player B to throw

If played regularly by players who know each other's degree of skill, a rough handicap system can be easily worked out. The lowest possible score for a round is 18 — the score every player should be aiming for, if not achieving. 'Par' for the course would be 54, ie 3 strokes per hole.
Tactics: Go for the trebles every time!

MICKEY MOUSE (TACTICS)
The numbers 1-20 are marked down the centre of the scoreboard and players throw for any of these targets in an attempt to score three hits on each (a treble counts as three hits and so on). Any number hit is marked with one cross per hit on that player's side of the scoreboard. (*See* Fig 26.) As soon as one player has three

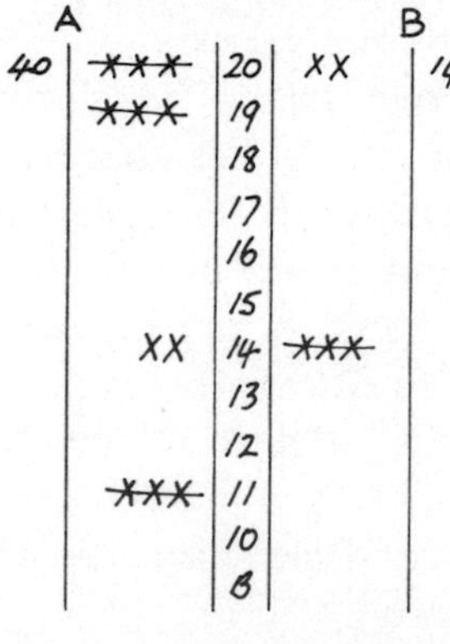

```
        A                        B
      40   ✗✗✗   20  ✗✗   14
           ✗✗✗   19
                 18
                 17
                 16
                 15
           ✗✗   14  ✗✗✗
                 13
                 12
           ✗✗✗   11
                 10
                  8
```

Fig 26 Typical Mickey Mouse scoreboard. Player A is scoring on 20, 19, and 11; B is scoring on 14

crosses against a number any more hits on it are scored in the normal way and totalled on the side of the scoreboard (eg hitting three 17s scores 51) until his opponent also acquires three crosses when the number is wiped off the scoreboard and takes no further part in the game. The player with the highest score at the end is the winner; the end of the game is reached when the player with the lower score has nothing left to score on. The bull is invariably included in the game at the bottom of the scoreboard: the outer bull counts as one hit and the inner bull as two.

A common variation is to omit the numbers 10 and 11 from the game entirely, so losing the easy 11-14 and 10-15 quadrants, and replace them with doubles and trebles (marked as D and T respectively on the scoreboard). These refer to *any* doubles and trebles regardless of their actual number eg 20x can be counted as one double or two 20s (though if 20s are off then it has to be counted as one double). Scoring is by their actual board value after any three doubles or trebles have been hit eg a shot in the 19t bed scores 57 if a player is scoring on trebles.

Tactics: This game is not also known as Tactics for nothing! There are two basic approaches: the first is to concentrate on building up a high score and then knocking off all those numbers your opponent can score on; the second approach is to get scoring on as many different numbers as possible and *then* start building up a good score. A player should be ready to chop and change between these two approaches during the course of a game, depending on the run of play and must rely on his own judgement when to do so. Since a game is often won or lost on the last few throws if the bull is left to the very end some players prefer to start off by going for it, hoping to get three quick bulls to give them a distinct advantage later on. Also, if you do miss the bull you stand a good chance of hitting one of the other scoring numbers. This slightly unorthodox tactic often produces the desired result of winning the game – as well as disconcerting more conventional players!

NOUGHTS AND CROSSES

The scoreboard is marked out in noughts and crosses fashion with any nine numbers filled in at random (1-9 or 10-18 are commonly used). A variation is to place the bull in the centre.

Each player aims to hit the *double* of any of the numbers on the scoreboard. When he achieves a hit his initial is written in its place and that number passes out of play. If the bull is being used then the *inner* must be hit for it to count. The first player to make a straight line of three initials in any direction noughts and crosses fashion, wins the game. (*See* Fig 27.)

Tactics: Go for the number in the centre of the grid first of all as this, if hit, will give you a choice of four different possible winning lines. If your opponent hits it before you then switch to one of the corner numbers to give you two possible lines (and knock out one of your opponent's). In short, adopt the tactics one would use in playing paper Noughts and Crosses (or, in the USA, Tic Tac Toe).

7	2	5
3	1	9
8	4	6

R	2	M
3	R	9
8	M	R

Fig 27 Typical Noughts and Crosses scoreboard (left) at the start and (right) at the end of the game

ROUND THE BOARD (ROUND THE CLOCK)

There are many different variations on this simple game; the best is that which suits the skill of the players involved. In its most basic form each player throws at the number 1 and as soon as he scores a hit he moves to the 2 and so on. Singles, doubles and trebles merely count as an ordinary hit. After the 20 comes the final shot of the bull (inner or outer). The first player to go 'round the board' wins the game.

In the more common game the doubles and trebles count at their normal face value if that amounts to 20 or less so that, for example, if a player shoots for 5 and hits 5t, his next dart will be for 16. If he then hits 16t he just goes on to 17. Harder variations are going round on doubles or trebles only and finishing with an outer then an inner bull. In some areas players have to score a double before they start on the 1 and then must finish on their and/or their opponents' double; elsewhere the last shot is for the 50 or two 25s in three darts.

A traditional throw in this game is a 'sergeant' or 'soldiers': if a player scores with all three darts of his throw then he is allowed a second turn on the board. (In Manchester, where the game is known as Slip-up, scoring with the *last* dart of the three earns another turn.) If this rule is applied it is possible for one player to go right round the board without his opponent getting a look in; if this happens then he – the opponent – is allowed an equal number of darts to try to draw or even win the game.

Tactics: The best combination of shots in the usual game is 1x-3t-10x, bull. If you cannot achieve this then aim for useful shortcuts such as 9x or 6t so that you have to go through as few of the numbers between 10 and 20 as possible.

SCRAM

The player to throw first is the 'stopper' and the other player is the 'scorer'. The stopper tries to land a dart in each number between 1 and 20 and so cross it off the scoreboard; the scorer meanwhile attempts to score on any numbers still left in the game. When all the numbers are gone the two players swop roles and repeat the process. The person with the highest score wins the game.

Doubles and trebles can either be counted as part of their numbers while scoring double and treble that number or as separate beds to be stopped in their own right.

Tactics: Both the stopper and scorer should start on the high numbers and work downwards.

A		B
X	1	XXX
XXX	2	XX
XXX	3	XXX
	4	XX
XX	5	
	6	XXX
XXX	7	X
XX	8	X
XXX	9	XX

Fig 28 Typical Shove Ha'penny scoreboard halfway through a game

SHOVE HA'PENNY

The numbers 1-9 are written in a column down the centre of the scoreboard; the players endeavour to score three of each in any order or combination, marking hits against the side of the appropriate number on the scoreboard with a cross. (*See* Fig 28.) Doubles and trebles count two and three respectively. The first player to complete his side of the scoreboard wins the game.

As in shove ha'penny proper, the catch in the game is that if a player scores *more* than three of a number during the course of play then the extra points are given to his opponent – though

they cannot be used to complete a player's score to win the game.
Tactics: No special tactics needed.

SNOOKER
Yet another two-player game based on a different sport. In this
case snooker ball values are allocated to different numbers on the
dart board — knowing how to play snooker is a great advantage
in understanding what is to follow. If you want to be really
fastidious, the numbers are set out on the scoreboard in positions
corresponding to those of the balls on a snooker table but a
simpler system such as that illustrated in Fig 29 will suffice. Ball
values are of course as for snooker.

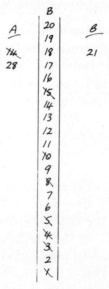

Fig 29 Typical Snooker scoreboard with seven reds gone

During play a red ball (1-15) is potted by scoring three of that
number in three darts or less, doubles and trebles counting as
two and three respectively. If a player succeeds in doing this he
then has to nominate one of the colours (16-bull) and has a fresh
throw of three darts at it. If that colour is potted then he has a go
at another red, and so on until the 'break' ends.

When a red is potted its number is erased from the scoreboard;

colours are returned to the 'table' until they are potted in the final sequence after all the reds have gone. Foul strokes are penalised thus: missing a red (ie not scoring a single hit in three darts) − 4 points away; missing a colour or potting a colour instead of a red − the loss of 4 points or the value of the colour, whichever is the greater: hitting a colour instead of a red, or hitting a colour not nominated − the same.

The highest score at the end of the game wins the 'frame'. Tactics: It is probably best to play safe and aim for the 'pink' (20) rather than the 'black' (bull) after potting a red since the difference of 1 point is more than compensated for by the easier target.

Games for more than two players

The following group of games are best played by a number of players, within the limits imposed by the nature of the game itself and the space and time available. They can still be played by just two people but their enjoyment value is usually found to be directly proportional to the number of participants! Each player is on his own against all the others.

Again, I have added notes on recommended tactics.

BIG 6 (FOLLOW-ON)

The first player throws for the 'big 6' − the larger single bed of the number 6. He is allowed three darts in which to hit it − failure to do so means the loss of a life and he has to try again. If however he hits it first dart then he has, in the next two darts, to hit any other bed (or indeed big 6 again if he wishes) − failure to do so again means the loss of a life. Hitting the big 6 with the second dart of his throw gives him just one dart with which to hit another bed whilst hitting it with the last dart of the three entitles him to another *three* at a new target.

The new bed hit by a successful player becomes the target in turn for his follower who has to hit in a similar manner to that outlined above − the waiting players usually shout out the bed to be aimed at eg 'little 3!' or 'double 1!' When a player loses all his lives then the target he was throwing for is passed on to the next player in line until only one, the winner, is left in the game.

Tactics: It should be obvious that the 'big' numbers are the easiest to hit, but they are also the easiest to leave the next person. The tactical skill called for involves important decisions concerning the target you set. Remember, *you* have to hit it first. If you have three darts, try for one of the traditionally 'difficult' doubles such as 3x or 5x with the first two and for the bull with the last if they miss. If you have two darts, use one for the double and the second for the bull. One dart left – go for the bull so that if you miss, at least you will set one of the 'small' numbers. And remember – darts bouncing out do not count even when setting a new target: if a dart bounces out you still lose a life.

HALVE-IT

The scoreboard is marked out as in Fig 30 with the players' initials at the top of the vertical columns. Players throw in turn for the first number (12); the total score value is then entered below the appropriate player's initial (eg 24, 48 or whatever). They then throw for the 13 and so on down the board, including the any doubles and any trebles shots, ending on the bull.

	A	B	C	D
12	24	12	*	12
13	50	25	13	38
14	78	67	27	66
D	118	34*	14*	68
15	148			
16				
17				
T				
18				
19				
20				
B				

Fig 30 Typical Halve-it scoreboard; player B to throw

Scores on subsequent throws are added to a player's running total; if nothing is scored then the total is halved with odd numbers being rounded up for this (eg 71 halved is 36). Bulls count as 25 or 50 as normal. It is customary to mark halved scores with a star.

The player with the highest score at the end wins the game — and the game is more often than not decided on the very last round of throws. If two players tie then the one with the fewer halved scores wins. It should be played for money to add a touch of real competition to it and this is normally done by each player chipping in a small stake at the beginning and a similar amount at the end for each star collected, winner taking the kitty.

Tactics: No special tactics are needed; most players though in this type of game where doubles and trebles are called for find it easiest to aim for the numbers on the sides of the boards (ie 6 or 11) so that any drifting of the dart up or down is still likely to score.

KILLER

Each player throws one dart with his 'wrong' hand until everyone has hit his 'own' number. No two players can have the same number. These are then marked on the scoreboard next to the players' initials. The game proper now commences with people in turn trying to hit the double of their own number; when they succeed in doing this they then go for any of the other players' doubles. Whenever one of these is hit that player loses a life. A player going for someone else's double is known as a 'killer' and the fact is denoted for all to see and fear by a large K chalked next to his number on the scoreboard. (*See* Fig 31.) If a killer hits his own double then he too must lose a life. The last player left in the game is naturally the winner.

```
A   3   K   ///
B   19      /
C   6   K   ///
D   14      //
```

Fig 31 Typical Killer scoreboard; A and C are 'killers' and B and D have lost
    lives

A common variation is that killers can only go for non-killers' doubles until everyone has become a killer. This makes for an even more vicious game, but then you don't play Killer if you don't want to know who your friends really are.

Tactics: Try to get a 'good' number at the very start – and by 'good' I mean one that will be difficult for the others to hit: 19, 3, 17, 5 or 1 are usually the best for this. If necessary, put in a little 'wrong' hand practice on the sly. During the game itself, try to eliminate the best players first.

BLIND KILLER

One of my personal favourites, this is a more subtle version of Killer and a pack of cards is needed to play it. The word 'Blind' refers to the gambling sense of unseen rather than unseeing for the attraction of the game is that, at first, no one knows whose double is what. This is done by selecting a number of cards from the pack on the following basis: Ace, 2, 3 etc equal to the number of players; it adds to the game to include one or two extra cards as 'floaters' just to confuse the issue. Players then throw for any double and when they hit one they become a killer and select one of the cards (which should be set-out face down) without showing it to the others. That card value (Ace, 2, 3, etc) is then their own double which, if hit by another killer, loses a life. Lives are marked on the scoreboard against the numbers used, not the players' initials – *see* Fig 32. When a number has lost all its lives then the player holding the corresponding card has to own up and drop out of the game. Last one left in is the winner.

```
1    ///
2    //
3    ///
4    //
5    /
6    ///
```

Fig 32 Typical Blind Killer scoreboard; the numbers 2, 4 and 5 have lost lives

Tactics: A great deal of bluff (not to mention skill) is needed to play this game and win since players will gang-up to knock off a certain double – especially if they think that a more skillful player has it. The less people you can get throwing at your double the better your chances; if you just plug away at one number until it is knocked off, then another, you will make it more difficult for the others to guess what number you have. An alternative approach is to go for any of the numbers in random order, slipping in the odd 'wide' shot at your own as a bluff. Sheer luck also plays an important role in this game since if you pick up one of the 'easy' numbers such as 4, 6 or 8 you suffer a distinct disadvantage from the very start since these tend to be the doubles most people go for first. Also, a number can be knocked off before anyone has picked up that card, which means you go straight out of the game if you do!

OVERS AND UNDERS

As its name suggests, there are two versions of this game. In both, each player has to score better than the previous player (or equal his score) or else he loses a life. The first player can throw whatever score he likes. If Overs (also known as Coach and Horses) is being played then successive players have to throw a higher (or equal) score; if Unders is played then everyone has to score equal or less. Failure to do so in either game results in the loss of a life and the next person has that new score to aim at with his three darts. The last one left in the game is the winner.

Games tend to be played in pairs with one Overs followed by one Unders. The latter is by far the more deadly of the two since non-scoring darts carry an automatic penalty of 25!

Tactics: Whenever possible play safe so as to achieve the necessary score with the minimum of risk. Concentrate on staying *in* the game rather than putting someone else *out* – they will quite easily do that for themselves.

	A	B	C
4	1	2	2
1	4	6	4
12	7		
10			
1			
3			
17			
11			
4			

Fig 33 Typical Oxo scoreboard; player B to throw

OXO

This curiously named game somewhat resembles Shanghai (see below). If there are less than five players each throws his three darts 'wronghanded' at the board until all three score; if five or more play the game then they only throw two darts. The numbers hit (doubles and trebles just count as the single) are chalked up on the scoreboard; if a number has been hit more than once then it is chalked up more than once. Players then throw for each number in turn to score on the basis of a single – 1, a double – 2 and a treble – 3 regardless of the face value of the number. Highest score after all the numbers have been aimed at wins the game. (*See* Fig 33.)

A variation is that instead of rethrowing a dart that has landed off the board during the first stage of the game, the surround to the scoring area of the board is used as a 'number' in its own right.

Tactics: No special tactics needed.

SHANGHAI

Players throw in turn for the number 1, scoring normal face value for their three darts. They then repeat the round on 2, 3 and so on up to 7. Highest total score at the end of the game wins.

Those are the basics. There is however a special shot that will automatically win the game on any number: scoring 'Shanghai' – hitting the single, double and treble of that number (in any order). A slight catch here is that if a player performs this feat

	1	2	3*	4	5*	6	7*
A	4	10	19	19	39		
B	2	4	—				
C	2	6	12	20			
D	3	7	13	25			
E	1	1	—				—
F	2	4	13	33			
G	1	3	6	6			

Fig 34 Typical Shanghai Scoreboard; C to throw. Players B and E have failed to score on 3 and dropped out

the following players in the round still have a chance to throw and if any one else matches it then the game continues.

One variation on the basic game is to play up to 9, especially if there are only two players. A more common variation is to 'Shanghai' players out of the game if they fail to score at all on the 3, 5 or 7 (and the 9 if used). This old slang expression for press-ganging no doubt gives the game its name from which in turn the Shanghai shot of single, double and treble has been taken. (*See* Fig 34 for a typical game scoreboard.)

Tactics: Go for Shanghai whenever possible – everyone else will be!

Team games

The next pair of games, although possible with only two players, are best enjoyed as team games. Both are examples of games cribbed from other sports – both, not surprisingly, team games in their own right. Neither calls for any special tactics beyond the obvious.

CRICKET

The scoreboard is marked out with a column for runs and a column for ten wickets as illustrated in Fig 35. The two captains (essential in team games so that you can always have someone to thank you for your efforts when you win and someone to blame when you lose) bull-up or toss a coin to see who has the choice of bowling or batting first. And as anyone who has played this game before well knows, this choice is more crucial than it sounds.

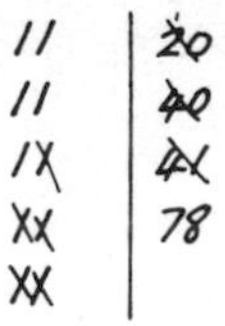

```
//    20
//    40
/X    4X
XX    78
XX
```

Fig 35 Typical Cricket scoreboard: 78 for 5

The bowling side opens the game with their first player throwing for the bull. Any scored (inner –2, outer – 1) claims the corresponding number of wickets and these are erased from the scoreboard. The opening batsman then throws, aiming for a high score since 'runs' are only scored above and beyond 40 eg a total of 54 on the dartboard counts as 14 runs. Then the next bowler, next batsman, going round and round through the players until either all the wickets have been taken or the batting side 'declares', satisfied with its score. The bowling side then has its innings, attempting to beat the other side's score. If time permits, a two-innings match makes for a fairer game.

To carry the cricket comparison further there are a number of additional rules. A batsman 'hitting his own wicket' (ie the bull) is automatically out. A bowler landing a dart outside the trebles ring gives that score away as 'wides'. Darts bouncing out are generally ignored though those that stick off the scoring area — from bowlers — count as 25 extras away.

FOOTBALL

A very simple game. Opposing players throw in turn, as in Cricket, with the object of hitting the inner or outer bull. When someone does so, he and the rest of his team then throw for any double which, if hit, counts as a 'goal'. Meanwhile the opposing team continues to aim for the bull which, if hit, gives them possession of the 'ball' so that they can now shoot for goals. So play goes back and forth with the ball constantly changing sides until one team wins the match by scoring a total of 10 goals.

East End board games

Whilst several of the preceding games can be played on the East End board, there are three others which are specifically intended for it. Details of these are outlined below.

FIVES

Broadly speaking this is the same as All Fives played on the London board. It is traditionally played up to 61 and scored on a crib board, pegging out exactly at the end. It tends to be a very fast game since anything scored has to be a multiple of 5 by the very nature of the board.

FIVES AND THREES

This corresponds to the dominoes game of the same name and is a development of Fives. Here scores divisible by 3 are also counted — in dominoes fashion so that a board score of 15 is reckoned as $(5 \times 3)+(3 \times 5) = 8$; 30 as $(5 \times 6)+(3 \times 10) = 16$ and so on. Keeping score is the same as for Fives.

305, 505 ETC

This is the standard game for the East End board and is identical to the London board's 301, 501 etc except for the different starting total necessitated by the board's unique numbering system.

Games for other boards

Most of the games described above can be adapted for playing on boards other than the London pattern. Sometimes the game becomes harder if, for example, the bull is smaller; sometimes a game loses much of its point by such a transfer — Shanghai for example on a board without trebles. A little thought and experiment however will soon show just what can or cannot be played on any particular regional board.

It should be stressed that all the games described in this chapter are as I have learnt them and are named as I know them. This is *not* to be taken as meaning that this is categorically how they should be played or indeed what they ought to be called; I have tried to include the more common variations on them and am glad to know that they are played in different ways and under different names in different places. Such variety adds to the charm of pub darts.

Part IV:
The evolution of darts

10 The history of the game

Ten years ago darts was just another pub game, played for the fun of it, with local leagues for the more dedicated players and – every dart throwers' annual dream of glory – the *News of the World* Championship. Today all that has changed. To be sure that same solid, widespread national base is still there: an estimated 6-7 million people in Great Britain regularly play the game, making it the most popular participant sport in the country (outstripping even fishing). But now we have entered the age of the professional, the tournament circuit, national teams and international matches. Darts is big money, not only for its top players but also for its sponsors and mushrooming equipment manufacturers. It is the difference between Sunday soccer in the park and the World Cup.

Here I have to take my own personal stand. While I recognise the place of 'top flight' darts I believe that this is not really what the game is all about; far from it. Darts at the highest level might well represent the standard of excellence towards which we lesser mortals humbly aspire; but the lower levels on which we play are the *real* home of the game. The pub or club is the true setting for darts, played not for money or grand trophies but simply for the joy of it. The most enjoyable games I have ever played took place in two pubs (both incidentally in Wales) during extended lunch-hours when I should have been more gainfully occupied elsewhere!

The dull idea of 'standardization' has even overtaken many of our pubs and darts has not escaped the general rule. This book is therefore not only a tribute to the game as a whole but also a record of the fascinating aspects of it to be found up and down the country before they are swept away and forgotten by the tide of conformity. Modern darts may be modern darts the world over but I for one should always like to think that, on either side of the Pennines for example, the game is still played in the local fashion. Long may such traditions continue.

In the beginning

It is impossible to pluck a date from the pages of history and state categorically when the game originated. As with so many sports and pastimes, the origins of darts can be traced further and further back until the earliest history of man is reached.

If we go back to the dawn of man as a thinking creature, some 3-4 million years ago according to the latest estimates, we can deduce from archaeological evidence the first use of stones and rocks as weapons for hunting and fighting. Their use must have gradually inculcated a practical knowledge of ballistics within the minds of our ancestors. Handed down through countless generations, that skill and awareness can still be seen today in a more peaceful form in such games as cricket, skittles, baseball and the like. (*See* Fig 36.)

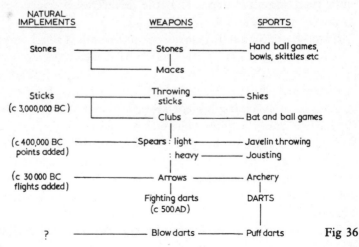

Fig 36

THE SPEAR

The first spears must have been simple straight lengths of stick shaped to a point at one end. With the discovery of fire, the fire-hardened wooden point came into widespread use (c400,000 years ago), followed by the invention of fashioned heads of bone, flint and later metal. Each step in the spear's development increased its value and it must have rapidly become a common weapon for both hunting and warfare.

The spear quickly evolved into two broadly distinct types: the light and the heavy. The light spear or javelin, often taller than a man, relied partly for its stability in flight upon the fact that it was shaken or spun round its axis before and during its delivery; its length also provided an aid to true flight. Still used for hunting in many parts of the world, its use in competition is doubtless as old as the weapon itself and has come down to us as the javelin of modern field athletics. A great many sports in fact originated in this way since, when there was nothing or no one to use one's weapons on, what could be more natural than friendly competition with them?

The heavy spear was, by contrast, a close-quarters weapon. Often exceedingly heavy, it relied upon the weight of its head and was primarily used as a stabbing weapon such as the Roman *pilum*. Although an excellent hunting weapon, the javelin was not ideally suited to battle since once thrown, that was that! Hence the predominance of the heavy spear as a weapon of war, either as a short stabbing spear or as the long pike and lance. What was needed was a more expendable missile: the arrow.

THE ARROW

The earliest known flint arrow heads have been found in North Africa and Europe and date back at least 50,000 years. Not only had the principle of the strung bow been discovered for projecting a very light spear further than it could be thrown by hand but, of more relevance to us, so had the idea of attaching flights to that spear in order to make it fly straight. And since the birds of the air could do so, what better material for such flights could be found than feathers?

So, still in prehistoric times, both ends of the dart had been separately invented: the point and the flight. What was now possible was a weapon that combined features from both the spear (point, weight and balance) and the arrow (point and flights) into an accurate, hand-thrown missile.

FIGHTING DARTS

After classical times the javelin was generally abandoned in Europe as a battle weapon and the short stabbing spear gave way to the sword which could cut as well as thrust. To be of any real use, a spear had to be thrown to kill one's enemy at a safe distance, but once thrown its use naturally ended. The obvious solution was to duplicate it in the same way as arrows: the dart was born. The credit for its invention is usually given to the Byzantine general Belisarius (c505-565), judged one of the greatest military minds in history. Under Emperor Justian I, Belisarius was responsible for defending the eastern Mediterranean empire and to do so armed his troops to the hilt. Some of his infantrymen carried three or four light javelins whilst the mounted bowmen carried three darts clipped behind their shield. Each dart was about 18in long, heavily weighted behind the head for penetration and flighted like an arrow for accuracy. (*See* Fig 37.) As part of their training, horsemen were required to practise throwing these darts at targets. It is not improbable to assume that games were played, or at least some form of competition developed, during or after these bouts of practice.

Fig 37 Byzantine fighting dart

The use of these fighting darts did not pass unnoticed in the countries to the west though it seems that they were simply (and justifiably) regarded as poor rivals to the bow and arrow and were consequently never taken up to any degree.

BLOW DARTS

This section would not be complete without mention of a weapon which, although not directly involved in the evolution of the game of darts, does provide an extremely curious link with it and is undeniably a member of the general darts family. (*See* Fig 38.)

Fig 38 Blow dart

The weapon is the blow dart, a slender wooden or thorn needle about 9in long (or less), flighted at the rear end with a ball of fibre or similar device to serve the double purpose of steering the dart and providing an air-tight seal in the blowpipe. This latter is a straight, hollow tube of bamboo 6ft or more in length. The range of this weapon is not much over a hundred feet but since the darts are invariably tipped with lethal poison this defect (and the limited penetrating power achieved) is not all that important: if you can hit your quarry, you will kill it.

The blowpipe, of unknown age, was and is confined for serious use to the jungle regions of Asia and South America, where suitable stems for the pipes grow. It is an extremely ancient weapon and was brought to Europe by traders; its use was recorded in England as early as the fifteenth century as a method of hunting birds. As such it survived for at least three hundred years and can even be purchased today, though in a much humbler form: the peashooter. What is intriguing about this weapon is that while in this country, it too was adapted to a competitive game, puff-darts, described in more detail below.

Target archery

Central to the history of darts in Britain is the role of the longbow. The bow has been used in this country since prehistoric times and by the thirteenth century, as the longbow, it had become *the* English weapon for battle. For the next three hundred years it won fame and inspired fear far across Europe. The skill of its archers was the strength of the English army and that skill was only acquired through continual practice. That practice, deemed so imperative for the defence of the realm, was enforced by law: from the middle of the thirteenth century onwards various statutes compelled all freemen between the ages of fifteen and sixty to keep a bow and arrows and to practice with them on Sundays and Holy Days. A similar edict was passed in Scotland by James I applicable to males over the age of twelve. This exercise officially took place at special butts erected for the purpose and these consisted of earth or stone walls, somewhat similar to modern rifle butts, against which the target would be fixed. Little is known about these early targets except that, to judge from contemporary illustrations, they all roughly conformed to the general pattern of a disc about six inches in diameter centred on a large protecting board. Other types of target archery were also practised: the most important of these was prick- or clout-shooting — aiming at a small piece of cloth pegged through the centre to the ground.

By the sixteenth century, or some time during it, it seems that the butt and clout targets had become one and the same: a tightly-packed disc of straw covered with cloth. It had a central bull which replaced the 6in disc of the older target and the peg in the centre of the clout. It was portable and reusable. It was the direct ancestor of the modern dartboard and, like its descendant, had a diameter of some eighteen inches.

It should not be imagined that the practice of archery was as diligently pursued as it was supposed to be. A gradual decline set in during the fifteenth century following the English archers' greatest victory at Agincourt in 1415. Despite the Wars of the Roses later in the century the general populace abandoned it wholesale in favour of less strenuous pastimes such as bowls or skittles. The reasons for this are not hard to find: longbows were becoming expensive and, more importantly, the handgun, known in Europe for a hundred years, had followed the crossbow across the English Channel and was about to displace both.

The Tudor monarchs were especially concerned with the problem and did their best to preserve proficiency with the weapon that had helped to make England great. Henry VIII himself took a keen delight in target archery and instigated strong action to stop the rot, including compulsory ownership of bows and arrows and weekly practice at the butts; other games were expressly forbidden. Similar measures were again enacted across the border in Scotland. It was a valiant last-ditch action but in the end a futile one. By the close of the century, the handgun had decisively taken over and by the end of the Civil Wars in 1648, the days of the longbow as a weapon of battle in England were finished.

The legacy of the longbow was a considerable one. Although the fate of nations no longer depended upon their skill, archers still practised their art in English fields. From Tudor times target archery became more and more a recreation in its own right with the blessing of successive monarchs. Guilds were formed to keep the butts open, competitions were organised and, in general, the basis was laid for a sport which has altered little in principle to this day.

In the middle of the eighteenth century the sport all but died out, only to be vigorously revived in the last quarter of that century as a pastime of the leisured classes. And since the Prince Regent himself was an avid early nineteenth century enthusiast, society flocked to the butts.

Why is all this relevant to the game of darts? There are two reasons, one specific and one general. The specific reason is that up to this time the sport lacked any real form of regulation. Range and target both differed greatly at different butts. Then, with the sport's revival, came the standardisation of the target. These had employed a pattern of concentric rings around the original bull since at least the 1750s but the idea of giving these rings different scoring values is reputed to have been that of the Prince Regent, though more likely the idea was as old as the rings themselves since the one is of little use without the other. The resulting face was a 4ft diameter disc with four concentric rings of white (scoring 1), black (3), blue or inner white (5), red (7) and a gold central disc (9) nicknamed the 'bull's eye'. Thus was established a standard pattern of target upon which scores could determine the superiority of one archer over another rather than just relying on the former hit-or-miss approach. It was the principle upon which the dartboard could later be based.

The second, more general reason for the relevance of target archery to darts is in the nature of the sport itself. Even if only actively participated in by a limited number of people, archery at this date was firmly established in the national consciousness. Few people could imagine a time when there were not bows and arrows. Up to Tudor times there would have been few people who had not actually used one. Small wonder then that another, more harmless form of missile/target game should have become so popular and so widespread. Small wonder also that it should be known familiarly as 'arrows'.

An unlikely story

At this point we come up against the problems which must be faced by anyone who writes, however sketchily, on the history of darts. No one knows exactly how, when and why the game was invented, though reasonable suppositions can be made.

Modern accounts of the game propose two main theories. The first of these suggests that darts began with a group of bored archers on a wet afternoon throwing whittled-down arrows at the end of a beer barrel behind the counter of an inn. On the face of it this is a plausible theory – until one realises that if the head is removed from an arrow, the cut-down shaft would not stick in; if the flights were missing not only would the shortened arrow not fly straight but it is doubtful if the large head would be sharp enough to penetrate wood if thrown by hand; if a new head was put on however the arrow would still have to be weighted and balanced so as to fly true . . . the drawbacks to this explanation are so numerous that darts *cannot* have been invented in this way. Proponents of the theory have overlooked one very important fact: a dart is *not* a cut-down or even a miniature arrow, it is a miniature fighting dart. Which leads us to consider the alternative theory of the game's origin: the continuation and refinement of a game played with actual fighting darts.

Medieval darts

It is often stated in books dealing with darts that the game's history can be traced back to a medieval sport played with short, heavily weighted fighting darts. This confident statement does not however bear close examination. Firstly, in contradiction to other writers on the game, I can find no evidence to suggest that English archers of any period carried fighting darts, their use being principally confined to the eastern Mediterranean region (eg by Turkish mounted bowmen) and in the second place, the theory appears to be based solely upon two references to 'darts' in Joseph Strutt's *Sports and Pastimes of the People of England* published in 1801. Without naming the source of his information, Strutt states that

> In the twelfth century we are assured, that among the amusements practised by the young Londoners on holidays, was casting of stones, darts and other missive weapons. Bars of wood and iron were afterwards used for the same purpose . . .

Strutt's second reference is to a set of 'darts of Biscayan fashion richly ornamented' presented to Henry VIII by Anne Boleyn. From the first quote it is clear that the 'darts' were not used in any sort of target game but merely thrown (cast) for distance; what is also apparent from the whole context of Strutt's remarks is that 'darts' are in fact *spears* and indeed are so recognised by him and included with javelins under that term. Before the introduction of the modern game, 'dart' (or 'darte') was used simply as a synonym for a short spear or arrow – as in the phrase 'Cupid's darts'. The *Oxford English Dictionary* traces this meaning of the word 'dart' back to the early fourteenth century in England (and derives it from the Old French) and to search for the origins of the game amidst such misleading clues is a futile occupation.

A more likely story

There is however another way in which the history of the game can be investigated. Instead of starting in the distant past, we can trace instead the records of the game as far back in time as they go. The one drawback to this method of course is that while a mention of the game confirms its existence, no mention does not disprove it.

By adopting this course of action though, two rather surprising facts are quickly disclosed. The first is that in the definitive reference work on the etymology of the English language, the *Oxford English Dictionary*, the word 'dart' as applied to the modern game is traced back only as far as 1901 when an advertisement for 'Dart boards' appeared in the *Stationer, Printer & Fancy Trades' Register* for 1 June of that year. The second curious fact is that while a whole variety of games and pastimes can be easily traced back through various records to the Middle Ages and before, no mention of darts as we know it has yet been found. This has been either conveniently ignored or blatantly disregarded as being contrary to conventional theories about the game's origin.

What does this lack of positive evidence indicate? Close study of the subject forces one to the conclusion that darts is not a very old game at all and the question of the game's origin can be roughly answered. At the very beginning of this book is a quotation from E. Temple Thurston, an Edwardian writer, traveller and gentleman. He encountered the game in the Red Lion pub in the Oxfordshire village of Cropredy and to judge from his description of it he expected it to be as novel to his readers as it was to him. And this was well into this century!

Returning to the *OED's* first mention, I can find no work on games published during the nineteenth century which includes darts at all, apart from the reference by Strutt to medieval 'darts' already discussed. Nor can I find any record of it in accounts of preceding centuries; this is in marked contrast to the well-documented records of a whole range of allied pub games and pastimes such as cards, chess, bowls, skittles, shuffleboard, dice, quoits and so on. It is impossible to pretend that, in the face of such evidence, darts, by some strange freak of history, just happened to escape note for all that time. Nor can I trace any evidence to support the oft-quoted 'fact' that the Pilgrim Fathers played the game on the *Mayflower* during their voyage to America in 1620. In view of their beliefs and code of living it is extremely unlikely that they played any other sort of game either. And before them, even a search of the works of Shakespeare, who probably made reference to every game of his age, will reveal only the use of the word 'dartes' as meaning arrows or spears. A whole list of such non-citations could be made but the point is too obvious to labour: darts is a recent invention.

But how did the game begin? Only a theory can be offered. The game is no more than indoor archery, played with hand- as opposed to bow-launched missiles. As such it was a working-class imitation of the leisured classes' bow and arrow activities coupled with a desire, after the massive urbanisation of the Industrial Revolution, to retain some sort of link, however tenuous, with a rapidly vanishing rural way of life for many workers. Such a desire also accounts for the popularity of pigeon racing, dog-breeding and fishing in predominantly industrial areas. Argument as to whether the board originated as a slice of a log or the end of a beer barrel is secondary to this fact. In other words, the boards did not produce the game but rather were manufactured from any suitable item or material that was to hand. No doubt both barrel and log boards *were* used at some time or other; in the Potteries area of Staffordshire the material was, not surprisingly, clay.

The variety of different board patterns still existing today in different parts of Britain bears testimony to the game's origins. It is not surprising to find that the three principle varieties of board are named after, and found in, three great centres of population or industry – London, Yorkshire and Manchester. It is just possible that some primitive form of darts was being played in these areas early in the nineteenth century but if so it can only have spread after the railway age of the 1840s and 1850s – and then slowly and haphazardly. Thurston only discovered it in 1910 or thereabouts; Rupert Croft-Cooke, writing as late as the 1930s, states categorically that there were

practically no dartboards in Ireland, few, though an increasing number in Wales, and none whatever, as I very bitterly know, in Scotland . . . It is played little in the North of England, and here and there you will come on an arid city like Birmingham in which it is scarcely seen.

(R. Croft-Cooke, *Darts*, 1934)

In short then, darts is not an off-shoot of target archery but rather an imitation of it and, in the form in which we know it, dates from only the latter half of the last century at the outside. This is not to deny that earlier darts did not exist; since the principle of the dart had been known since before the Middle Ages, it is not surprising to find that at various times miniature versions of fighting darts were made. One of the most famous examples was that of the seventeenth-century French historian Paul Pelisson who, whilst imprisoned in the Bastille, fashioned some darts from wood and pins and threw then at the panelled ceiling of his cell. Such cases are definitely isolated instances though and there is nothing to suggest that any proper form of game was ever played with them.

One important question has so far been avoided: how did the segregated board originate? It is easy to assume that the first dartboards were of the ring type – derivations from the pattern used for archery. This is not a safe assumption at all though; undoubtedly boards such as the Norfolk or the Target are modelled on archery targets but do they necessarily predate the segmented boards? As far as I am aware the use of segments is not known on archery targets, nor is the idea of having high scoring areas (such as doubles on a dartboard) other than the bull. My contention is that the segmented board is as old as the ring board for the very good reason that it just does not make sense to put an archery target face onto a dartboard. Even the average player would have no difficulty in hitting the central area every time, say three or four scoring rings, and the rest of the board would be superfluous. The Norfolk board met this problem by being of small size overall but this still means that the *variety* of scores possible was extremely limited (4, 3 or 1 in fact) and hence the game must have been excruciatingly boring.

The segment pattern was therefore devised in order to utilise the whole scoring area of the board; perhaps the unknown genius responsible also devised the doubles ring as far from the bull as possible. Certainly the different numbering order of the segments used on different boards must have come from separate sources – but all make good use of the principle of alternating very high and very low numbers wherever possible. The end product is a board on which the whole face can and indeed must be used during a game. Possibly the idea of segments as opposed to rings did come from the radial cracks which would develop in a drying-out log end; I am more inclined to think that it came from the spokes of a wheel, a far commoner sight.

Puff-darts

Mention must be made here of a curious game that was apparently played in Sussex pubs around the 1880s, according to a reference and photograph in the *Countryman* magazine, Winter 1947 issue. Known as puff-darts, it was based on the ordinary game of darts but used blow darts and a miniature board. The darts were about 1in long and blown from a 3ft tube; the board was made of wood with a scoring area some 6-7in in diameter. Curiously the board's numbering system is a copy of the Manchester pattern and not, as one would have expected, the standard London pattern usual in the south. Judging from the photograph of the board it is quite possible that it is simply a Manchester board a long way from home!

It has been claimed that this old game is a descendant of a children's pastime mentioned by Strutt as dating back to at least the sixteenth century: blow-point. According to Strutt, this *possibly* consisted of 'blowing an arrow through a trunk at certain numbers by way of lottery'. Even if it was not, the idea of such a game was clearly not unfamiliar to him since, as already mentioned in this chapter, the blowpipe had been known in England for some three centuries before his time. It would be natural for it to be taken up as a plaything by children (and others), using a variety of targets including, in time, ordinary dartboards. As a pub game though a full-sized board would have presented too easy a target, hence the introduction of a miniature version. A modern parallel is the practice of using a dartboard as a target for airgun darts.

According to *The Dart* magazine of 8 February 1948, an exponent of the game was to be found in the Lincolnshire village of Pinchbeck. He was apparently quite capable of hitting the board from a distance of 40ft! It would seem therefore that the game was in fact more widespread than has been generally thought though to the best of my knowledge it has been extinct for a good many years. A fascinating postscript to the story is provided by Sean Tracy in *A smell of broken glass* published in 1973. Writing of his life as a publican in London, Tracy describes a modern form of puff-darts as played by the writer Laurie Lee. Using a 2ft plastic tube and old-fashioned full-size wooden darts wound with sticking plaster to form an air-tight seal in the blowpipe, Lee was no mean exponent of this odd variant of the normal game!

The modern game

The ramifications of World War I stretched far and wide, affecting a host of different matters. The sheer mixing of men, and their leisure activities, from all over Britain must have done more to hasten the spread of darts than in any other comparable period of time. It was also the time when the Americans encountered the game in a big way (although it had already crossed the Atlantic with the mass emigrations of the late nineteenth century). At the same time we find the first literary reference to the game so far traced. The setting is a flower show:

> there were coconut shies and many ingenious prize-giving shooting and dart-throwing and ring-throwing stalls, each displaying a marvellous array of crockery, clocks, metal ornaments and suchlike rewards.
> (H.G. Wells, *Mr Britling Sees It Through,* 1916)

A scene not far removed from the modern fairground!

In passing, it is interesting to note that the last recorded use of darts in warfare in Europe occurred during the early days of World War I. Both the French and the English dropped large steel ones from their aeroplanes; the former country used them against the German infantry while the latter used them against the more vunerable gas-filled Zeppelins until the development of reliable tracer bullets.

After the war years it became clear that the number of club teams and casual players was growing rapidly and, as with other sports, some sort of national body would have to be set up if the game was to become more than just a local pastime. Accordingly, in 1924 the Licensed Victuallers Association (who had been 'responsible' for the game up till then simply because of its close ties with licensed premises) established the National Darts Association. One of the NDA's first acts was to organise an all-London tournament sponsored by the *News of the World* newspaper. Nothing like it had ever been attempted before and no one knew for certain just how well it would be received. In the event it proved a great success: eliminating heats were held during the 1927-8 season (like football and rugby, competitive darts is traditionally a winter sport) and the winner, out of 1,010 entrants, was C. 'Sammy' Stone of the New South-west Ham Workingmen's Club who triumphed over W.M.C. Haigh of Hayes at the Holborn Hall final.

From that humble beginning the *NoW* competition has gone from strength to strength. In the 1935-6 season the Home Counties (Surrey, Kent, Essex, Hertfordshire, Buckingham-shire, Berkshire and the rest of Middlesex) were included for the first time; in 1936-7 a separate Welsh tournament was organized, followed in 1937-8 by one for Lancashire and Cheshire. The next year saw similar regional titles for Yorkshire, the North of England and the Midlands while the Home Counties area was expanded to embrace the whole of southern England. The final of this division, held in the Royal Agricultural Hall, Islington, packed in a crowd of 14,534 spectators – still an all-time record for a darts match.

It was about this time that the first book devoted solely to darts was published (1936). Written by Rupert Croft-Cooke, a professional writer of the period, and simply entitled *Darts*, it was an insubstantial pocket-sized volume, very lightweight in content and with an extremely annoying patronising style to boot. What is important about it though is the valuable picture it gives of the status of the game at that time. I have already quoted from it in the previous chapter with respect to the geographical spread of the game; other remarks in it indicate that, writing more than twenty years after Thurston, Croft-Cooke regarded darts as a game with which he too did not expect his readers to be very familiar. For him it was an out-of-the-way pub game, much on a par with skittles or shove-ha'penny, unknown to anyone who had never ventured inside a public bar. The very fact that the book was produced at all though clearly shows that darts was starting to boom and someone at least was eager to cash in on the trend. It perhaps became truly respectable at that May 1939 *NoW* final when broadcast by the BBC for the first time. Social acceptance indeed!

On the other side of the Atlantic the game had reached a similar position – a fact delightfully illustrated by a scene from the 1939 film *Son of Frankenstein* in which a highly agitated Baron Frankenstein (Basil Rathbone) challenges the suspicious Krogh (Lionel Atwill) to a game. The policeman accepts and, not to be bothered by such a minor matter as possessing only one hand, with a gloriously bizarre gesture sticks the darts into his wooden arm before his throw!

The post-war years

During the years of World War II the game was literally carried all over the globe. What the first war had done for darts in Britain, the second did for the whole world and it can be held primarily responsible for darts' popularity overseas. In Britain the overall organisation of the game continued to develop. The *NoW* championship, suspended during the hostilities, was resumed in the 1947–8 season on a new basis: just one tournament covering the whole of England and Wales. It was an obvious and logical step and the popularity of the game can be judged by the fact that there were no less than 289,866 entries for the competition that year. It had become, in effect, the unofficial world championship of the sport. (It is a significant reflection on the slow spread of the game in Scotland that that country was not included in the tournament until the 1971–2 season.) A complete list of *NoW* winners is given in Appendix 3.

It was the decade after the war that saw the rise of the darts professional or semi-professional. Before the 1940s the game had been played strictly between friends or rivals for the sake of points, pints, a title or two, or just for the sheer fun of it. In the gloomy years during and after the war people were in need of good, cheap entertainment, and what better than an evening spent down at the pub or club watching a top-flight display of darts skill? The exhibition player had arrived.

Without a doubt the two greatest names on this new 'darts circuit' were those of Jim Pike and Joe Hitchcock. Pike had been the *NoW* London area champion in 1939 (and runner-up in the London & South of England final) before turning professional; he had in addition no less than thirty-six other major titles to his credit. He captained the *News of the World* Four on their exhibition and charity tours while Hitchcock led their opponents, the St Dunstan Four. Although Hitchcock's competition record is not as impressive as Pike's, he was the born exhibition player, delighting in 3,001 marathons and nail-throwing displays. These latter feats he performed with sharpened 4in nails, playing (and beating) opponents using ordinary darts, knocking bottle tops and matchboxes off people's ears and noses, taking cigarettes out of their mouths and the like. But, gimmicks apart, his prowess at 3,001-up demonstrated his superb consistency in churning out 100+ shots throw after throw after throw. It was little wonder that he normally won his games by margins of 1,000 or more!

Pike was no mean performer either and two of his records still stand today: three games of 301 (without an opponent) in $2\frac{1}{2}$ minutes, set at Broadcasting House, Birmingham, in 1952 and going round the doubles at arm's length (in numerical order) in just $14\frac{1}{2}$ seconds at Newmarket in 1944.

THE NDAGB

The old NDA had not been reformed after the war and the need for a new overall body to govern the sport was evident. So, in 1953, the *People* newspaper (later the *Sunday People*) helped found such an organisation: the National Darts Association of Great Britain (briefly called the National Darts Union) with a council elected from representatives of the game from each county. In turn the NDAGB organised the Lord Lonsdale competition, a team trophy first contested in the 1938–9 season, revived after the war in 1946–7 and run as an annual event by the *People*.

Although now possessing a degree of national control, the growth of competitive darts was much the same as before and indeed suffered a setback after 1962 when the *People* withdrew its support from the Lord Lonsdale cup for financial reasons. Although held in 1963–4, the competition was not successfully revived until 1966–7 by the NDAGB, and with the previous eight-man teams reduced to six. But in the meantime a second team competition had appeared on the scene: the Nodor Challenge Cup sponsored by the darts equipment firm of that name. From a small beginning, confined to just Essex, in 1957, it had spread to four counties by 1958 and had doubled in size in both of the following two years; in 1961 it was open to four-man teams from the whole of England and Wales.

On a more modest scale, but indicative of the outside interest being shown in the game, a competition within a competition was sponsored by the cigarette firm of John Player & Sons. Competitors in the *NoW* championship, from 1966 to 1970, had to score as many 6s as they could with six darts. The idea was to promote the cigarette brand Player's No 6 and in 1969 Eddie Brown, winner of the *NoW* title, took first prize (with only seven 6s) in this mini-competition as well! At the same time local and regional tournaments throughout the country were also attracting local sponsors, usually the breweries of the area.

Darts today

Unquestionably the greatest boost to the game has come in the 1970s with its introduction to television. Just as snooker has become 'respectable' in Britain as a direct result of televised competition, so darts has been broadcast to millions of viewers who had previously regarded it as an amusement to while away an idle hour. Once an audience of television size is attracted to the game, there is bound to be immense commerical interest. With the televising of the *NoW* final, the annual 'Indoor League' pub games competitions on ITV and other special events (such as the 1977 Silver Jubilee international team tournament), darts is now a regular feature of sports programmes. It is of course greatly helped by being ideally suited to the medium with its short games and easy-to-follow action, and its static indoor nature also means that events are comparatively cheap to cover. My one regret is that 'Indoor League' has abandoned its original practice of using the Yorkshire board (the programme is made in Leeds) in favour of the London variety. 'Standardisation' of the game is one of the avowed aims of the NDAGB: writing in his book *Darts* (1973) Tom Barrett reports the NDAGB's chairman, Johnny Ross, as regretting that the 'one board, one set of rules' ideal had not yet been achieved. In Ross's estimation the process would take another five or ten years. In a country that values individuality, it is to be hoped not.

The NDAGB meanwhile faces its own problems. Each county of England and Wales has its own Darts Association, above which are ten Area Darts Associations: London and Southern Counties, North Home Counties, Midlands, Eastern, Northern, North-west, West, Wales, Scotland and Ireland. Each area in turn elects to the national Executive Council which, every year, organises a whole range of team and individual national championships with the aid of outside sponsorship. In recent years however a rival body, the British Darts Organisation, has largely usurped the NDAGB's role. Led and inspired by its secretary, Olly Croft, the BDO co-ordinates a system of County Darts Organisations similar to that of the NDAGB; its whole policy is to actively promote the game as a major sport at all levels, rather than just administrate it. It organises county and area tournaments, county league matches and the like, and in the process has drawn in an immense amount of sponsors' money for these events. Its top tournament is the World Masters, inaugurated in 1975. Winners of this title to date are Cliff Inglis (1974), Alan Evans (1975), John Lowe (1976), Eric Bristow (1977, 1979) and Ron Davis (1978).

THE BDO
The BDO was formed in 1973, to run an inter-county league. Now it has outgrown that original aim and has since moved into equipment marketing and staging tournaments for other bodies

such as outside sponsors and television companies although the money received is ploughed back in prizes. The resulting rash of national tournaments must somehow be co-ordinated by the NDAGB and the BDO so that the present confused situation is clarified. (There are, for example, at present two 'British Opens' sponsored by different firms). By all means have as many tournaments as the sport will stand but there should be just one national individual title, one national team title. In the far richer game of golf there is only one British Open but several other big money events to fill out the season. This would no doubt mean relegating the *NoW* championship to 'second-class' status but the sport as a whole would benefit from such rationalisation in the long run.

THE SDA

In Scotland the picture is slightly different. Mention has already been made of the game's lack of popularity north of the border but this is now rapidly becoming a thing of the past. First included in the *NoW* championship in 1971–2, Scotland formed its own darts body, the Scottish Darts Association, at the same time and began its own national championships. In 1974 the SDA affiliated itself to both the NDAGB and the BDO and is growing in strength throughout the country.

WALES AND IRELAND

Within Wales there are a number of bodies involved in running the game: the Wales & Western region of the BDO, the Welsh Darts Organisation (affiliated to the World Darts Federation in its own right), the Wales Darts Association and the Wales Darts Federation. Some co-operation exists between these various organisations but the general impression is that the overall picture is unnecessarily complicated. Such confusion is, alas, typical of the British sports scene and arises from the differing political status of the United Kingdom and its component countries.

A somewhat similar state of affairs exists in Ireland. The Irish Darts Organisation is affiliated to the WDF and covers both Eire and Ulster. Not affiliated to the WDF is the Ulster Federation of

Darts, founded in 1977, which serves the 31 official leagues of the province.

HOME INTERNATIONALS

Organised by the BDO, the British Home Internationals have been going since 1973 and players are picked from the county level for a national squad. Results to date are:

Year	Winners	Runners-up	Venue
1973	England	Wales	Bristol
1974	England	Wales	London
1975	Wales	England	Cardiff
1976	England & Scotland	Wales	Dundee
1977	Wales	England	Swansea
1978	England	Wales	Morecambe
1979	England	Wales	Leith

Ireland has yet to reach the first two places.

Other inter-county matches have been played but the situation is complicated by the fact that the NDAGB also runs an England team! A 'Great Britain' team has also occasionally appeared to take on Wales under the auspices of the Welsh Darts Federation.

INTERNATIONAL MATCHES

The 1970s, besides this heavy promotion at home, have also seen the introduction of international matches. This new aspect of the game began in October 1972 with a friendly match between Britain and the USA in the Trafalgar Tavern in Greenwich. The line-up of the two teams was:

Britain

Tommy O'Regan (NDAGB champion 1970, 1971, 1972)

Dennis Kilbourne (NDAGB runner-up 1972)

Alan Cooper (NDAGB Western Area champion 1972)

Alan Thomas (NDAGB Welsh champion 1972)

Abie Buckland (NDAGB Northern Home Counties champion 1972)

Paul Tunley (NDAGB Midland Area champion 1972)

Jean Smith (NDAGB Women's champion 1972)

Brian Netherton (*NoW* champion 1972)
Alan Evans (*NoW* runner-up 1972)
USA
Robert Thiede (North American champion 1971)
Jack Carr (West Coast champion 1972)
Jacqueline Egan (South Carolina and East Coast Women's
   champion 1972)

The result, after four men's pairs, one three-a-side and one
ladies' singles was a 5–1 win for Britain. Since then the number
of international matches has quickly increased as the game has
boomed on the Continent and in America and in many other
places overseas. Inevitably darts at this level has become too
'Americanised' with its garish team uniforms and emblems more
suited to a baseball park than an English pub. Surely the game
does not need this distracting razzmatazz or is it the price to be
paid for world status?

To bring the story up to date: in 1977 the WDF inaugurated a
World Cup competition for WDF member nations; held in
England that year the first four places were filled by (1st) Wales,
(2nd) England, (3rd) Ireland and (4th) New Zealand. Destined
to be a biennial event, there is a strong possibility that it will in
future be hosted by different countries in turn. Inaugurated in
1978 was the Europe Cup with the competition being held in
Denmark to coincide with the Denmark Open. Eleven countries
took part and the first four places were taken by England,
Scotland, Wales and Ireland. British dart players may still lead
the world – but the opposition gets tougher every year.

Ladies' darts

Another aspect of the game's boom is the rapid rise in status of
ladies' darts. There is nothing new of course in the idea of women
playing darts – they have been doing so successfully for years –
but in certain quarters such female participation was definitely
not encouraged; since dartboards were usually only to be found
in the public bar and since these were traditionally (and in some
cases exclusively) males preserves, the ladies in the lounge bar
consequently had little opportunity to practise the sport.

In spite of the obstacles, ladies' teams were established and they flourished. Today, in an age which has at long last generally recognised the concept of sexual equality in opportunity, it is no longer headline news if a pub team includes a woman in its line-up. Only a few years ago such a story would have found a paragraph or two for itself in many papers. The increase in the number of tournaments all the way up to national level has not failed to provide for lady players and many events have their ladies section (and often ladies' pairs and mixed doubles as well). This is true the dart-playing world over; in Britain the impetus given to the game by the BDO has also encompassed ladies' darts and the county league structure for men is paralleled by a similar one for women. At the highest level women's teams compete on the international stage.

It would be true to say that at present the world's best male players are consistently better at darts than the leading female players. This is perhaps largely due to lack of experience and opportunity in the past since there seems to be no physical reason for any difference in ability. No doubt in time we shall see the closing of this gap with men and women competing on equal terms in a whole range of events, though if ladies-only competitions continue then it is only fair that men-only events do likewise.

11 Darts around the world

It would be impossible to write a book about darts without a strong British bias since, like cricket, it is a very English invention and its early history is consequently confined to the country of its origin. This is no longer the case; mention has been made concerning the export of the game overseas, both in war and in peacetime, and the present situation abroad deserves closer study.

The general picture is an interesting one and it has a number of parallels and contrasts with the world picture of cricket. The parallels (with certain exceptions) are that they are both strong in those countries where Britain once held sway; the contrasts arise from the fact that since darts really only spread abroad after World War II, with the British withdrawal it has never gained a serious foothold in either India or Pakistan – both of course strong cricketing nations. (Interestingly the game has caught on amongst members of the Asian community in Britain.) The major exception to this state of affairs is the USA where for some reason, darts has been taken up in a big way whilst other British sports such as cricket and rugby football have not. The minor exceptions are some of the European countries and Japan; the first case can best be explained by geographical proximity and, the second, by a conscious desire to take up Western sports, witness the great popularity in Japan of golf, baseball and in recent years, rugger. Above all, darts needs very little by way of space or other facilities to become established, and once established it appears to take root extremely quickly.

THE WDF

Many of these countries' official organising bodies are affiliated to the World Darts Federation, a body set up after the formation of the BDO in an attempt to regulate the game on an international level; the British influence here is clearly apparent from the fact that both bodies share the same Secretary.

The WDF was formed in 1976 after representatives of several countries got together in London at the Unicorn World Darts Championship for the specific purpose of establishing one international ruling authority for the game. The WDF then set about the task of approaching the various national darts organisations around the world to evaluate their claims to be most representative of the game in their particular country. The WDF then chose the most representative to become an affiliated member; at present twenty countries belong to the WDF, covering all the major dart-playing nations. One very important step on the road to standardising the game, at least at international level, was the decision taken at their meeting in December 1977 to adopt a throwing distance of 7ft 9$\frac{1}{4}$in (2.37m) and this move has been supported by the various members and is being put into effect. The Executive Council of the WDF meets during every World Cup tournament and also during the World Masters tournament every other year.

Set out below are notes on all those countries where darts has attracted an established and organized following; they are arranged in continental order. (Full details of their various national tournaments and champions, as well as of the bodies themselves, can be found in any of the yearbooks listed in the *Bibliography;* their addresses are also given in Appendix 2.)

Africa

SOUTH AFRICA

The only African country where darts takes its place in the world scene is South Africa. The game has been long-established there and the South African Darts Association was formed in 1957. Affiliated to it are eighteen Provincial Associations and annual closed and open championships are held. The SADA is an associate member of the WDF; the President of the WDF, Mr Shan David, is himself a South African.

America

CANADA

Canada is very much the poor relation of the USA when it comes to darts but even so the game is very popular in certain areas and the country has a governing body in the shape of the National Darts Federation of Canada. This was founded in 1977 to run a new open championship and is affiliated to the WDF; prior to 1977 the general overall control of the game was in the hands of the Canadian Darts Council.

USA

As in Canada, darts has been played informally in the USA for a number of years but has only made significant strides within the last decade or so. The national body, again affiliated to the WDF, is the American Darts Organisation which was established after a meeting of several interested enthusiasts in Detroit in 1975. Again as in Canada a national open championship is held annually along with a number of other big money events and the country is fast becoming a major venue for professional darts.

The ADO works through a total of nine Regions, each with its own Director, and below this level comes a wide range of State and local darts associations. The game's most dedicated following is probably to be found on the West Coast with California boasting at least a dozen sizeable associations; the East Coast however does not lag so far behind and in fact the sport is gaining in popularity from Alaska to Hawaii. Some forty associations are at present directly affiliated to the ADO comprising some 20,000 members – and this is by no means the sum total of dart players in the country.

The ADO's regional breakdown is as follows:

1 North California, Oregon, Washington, Alaska, Nevada, Utah, Montana, Idaho, Wyoming
2 South California, Arizona, New Mexico, Hawaii
3 Texas, Oklahoma, Mississippi, Alabama, Louisiana, Nebraska, Colorado, Kansas, Arkansas, Western Missouri

4 Ohio, Michigan, Kentucky, Tennessee, Western Pennsylvania, Indiana
5 District of Columbia, Virginia, West Virginia, Maryland,
North Carolina, South Carolina, Georgia, Florida
6 Eastern Pennsylvania, Delaware, South New Jersey
7 New York, North New Jersey
8 Massachusetts, Conecticutt, Maine, Vermont, Rhode Island,
New Hampshire
9 North Dakota, South Dakota, Upper Michigan Peninsular,
Wisconsin, Illinois, Minnesota, Iowa, Eastern Missouri

A lot of money is flowing into the game in the USA and every
year an increasing number of British professionals cross the
Atlantic for the lucrative tournaments and general exhibition
tours. The traffic is by no means purely one-way for many of the
top American players are becoming very well known in Britain
through various open events. The American national champion
is now invited to participate in the *News of the World* Finals and
in 1975 Conrad Daniels, one of the USA's most familiar faces in
British televised darts, won Yorkshire TV's Indoor League
competition.

OTHER TERRITORIES
Darts is building up a strong following in the Caribbean and
already governing bodies exist in the following islands:

Barbados – Barbados Darts Association
Guyana – Guyana Darts Association
Jamaica – Friendly Darts League
Trinidad – South Trinidad Darts Association

These bodies have yet to join the WDF but further to the north
the Bermuda Darts Organisation is affiliated.

Asia

HONG KONG
This tiny colony has of course strong ties with Britain and it is
not surprising to find that it boasts its own Darts Association for
the benefit of ex-patriates. It is affiliated to the WDF.

JAPAN

Darts really took off here in 1974 when the first league was formed. Up to then the game was purely a recreation for Westerners in just one or two pubs but, in typical Japanese fashion, when the locals adopted the sport they did so with a vengeance. In 1975 the Japan Darts Association (in Japanese the Nipon Darts Kyoka) was established and national and local championships organised; foreign skill has been quickly eclipsed by home-grown talent and, before very long, top Japanese players will be seen in major European and American tournaments competing on equal terms just as they do now in golf.

Also an associate member of the WDF, the JDA is responsible for running the Tokyo League and has been instrumental in helping to spread the game to other countries of south-east Asia.

SINGAPORE

Darts has been played in Singapore by the British for a good many years and its legacy was such that after the withdrawal of British forces in 1975 the Singapore Darts Association was formed (not as yet affiliated to the WDF) to carry on running the game.

Australasia

AUSTRALIA

In view of the steady flow of emigrants from Britain to Australia over the years it is not surprising to find that darts has been well established in this country for a very long time indeed. Today it claims to be, after Britain, the world's second major darting nation with over 60,000 registered players in some 5,000 leagues.

In many ways the recent history of the game here is very similar to that in Britain: for a long while it was confined to pubs and clubs until the late 1950s when it emerged as a sport at the State level. State championships were inaugurated as the game began to take off but the situation was unnecessarily confused by the fact that some States held what they termed 'Australian' championships where the participants actually all came from the one State! Matters were soon rectified for in 1962 the Australasian Darts Council was set up to co-ordinate the game at the national level and to organize proper national championships. Its member associations are:

Australia Capital Territory Darts Council
New South Wales Darts Council
New Zealand Darts Council
Queensland Darts Association
South Australia Darts Association
Tasmanian Darts Council
Victorian Darts Association
Western Australia Darts Association

Since 1964 a national championship (singles and team) has been held with a ladies' singles and team championship added in 1972 and a mixed-doubles event in 1976. Each member of the ADC plays host to the championships in rotation and, as in the USA, the national winner is invited to the *News of the World* final in London.

In 1976 a second body was established: the Darts Federation of Australia to conform with the requirements contained in the constitution of the WDF. It has the same membership as the ADC but without the NZDC and the two bodies have several officials in common.

FIJI

Darts in the Pacific islands might seem a slightly strange notion at first but when it is remembered that the Fijians are also dedicated rugger players the idea is not such a peculiar one. On a formal level the game here dates back only to 1975 though with the formation of the Suva Darts League. In the following year, backed by commercial sponsorship, national championships were inaugurated and run by the league from which has stemmed the national Fiji Darts Association.

NEW ZEALAND

The darts scene in New Zealand has developed in much the same way as it has in Australia; the governing body (backed by a government grant towards administrative costs) is the New Zealand Darts Council which was formed in 1956. At present it has fifty-four registered associations with a total membership of 7,000 players and, as in most countries, this figure is still growing annually. National men's and women's singles and pairs championships are held each year, together with a mixed pairs event and a junior championship for players under sixteen years of age.

The . New Zealand Darts Council has a seat on the Australasian Darts Council and is affiliated to the WDF in its own right.

Europe

Darts has been played in some European countries for several years but in others it does not appear to have caught on at all. Its main strongholds are in northern Europe and this is no doubt due to climatic reasons, the long winter evenings being conducive to the game. The principal dart-playing countries are listed below; all are affiliated to the WDF.

BELGIUM
The sport is administered here by the Belgian Darts Federation (Fédération Belgique de Dards) which was formed in 1959, which makes it the oldest national darts body in Europe outside the British Isles. Organised matches are run on a league basis by the BDF and there are eight such leagues consisting of some 2,500 players in all. Both open and closed championships are held each year.

DENMARK
The governing body here is the Danish Darts Union (Dansk Darts Union) which was founded in 1965. As in Belgium, both open and closed championships are held annually.

FINLAND
Another northern country where the game is building up a good

following is Finland; the game is controlled here by the Finnish Darts Union.

FRANCE

France is very much a newcomer to the darts scene but already has its own national body, the French Darts Federation (Fédération Française de Dards) formed in 1976. Only time will tell if the game catches on here to the extent that it has in Scandanavia.

GIBRALTAR

It is hardly strange to find that darts has a good, if tiny, following in Gibraltar; in many ways the situation is very similar to that in Hong Kong with some 300 players in the one major league. The sport is controlled by the Gilbraltar Darts Association and, besides open singles and doubles championships, various other sponsored tournaments are held every year.

MALTA

Again, because of its former strong ties with Britain, it is no surprise to find darts flourishing on this island as well. The national body is the Malta Darts Association and again annual open championships are held.

NETHERLANDS

The Netherlands can already boast some 1,500 league players in three major leagues even though the national body, the Netherlands Darts Association (Nederlanse Darts Bond), was founded as recently as 1975. An annual national team championship is held, together with an open singles event.

SWEDEN

Sweden is fast becoming the leading darts nation of Europe (outside Britain) and their national champion is now invited to take part in the *News of the World* final. In 1978 Stefan Lord, probably the country's most well-known player, actually beat all the home opposition to take the title!

The governing body is the Swedish Darts Association (Svenska Dartforbundet), founded in 1973, and some 5,000 players play in the two major leagues. A range of open and closed championships are held each year as well as a number of other sponsored events. Strong links exist between the darts fraternities of Britain and Sweden and this is evidenced each year not only by individuals competing in open events in the other country but also by national teams undertaking tours and international matches.

12 The future

Where do we go from here? Is there a limit to the growth of darts' popularity? Fads of the past decades, such as canasta or mah-jong, faded as quickly as they arose because – unlike darts – they lacked a wide enough level of support to sustain more than a passing interest. The recent craze for backgammon is going exactly the same way.

Promoted by television coverage and big-money sponsorship the game seems to go from strength to international strength. Some kind of international league or knockout tournament must surely be a likelihood, replacing the present assortment of friendlies and invitation matches. The World Cup has arrived; a European Cup is on the way. Ten years ago the suggestion that darts might become part of the Olympics would have been laughed out of court; today it is a serious proposal but would it help the game? Ten years ago too the idea that darts would develop like professional golf would have been met with ridicule; today it seems truer and truer with every new tournament – and even more so in the USA where the game is played with greater fanaticism and theatricality than in Britain. Golf has been played on the moon; darts too has literally gone out of this world, the occasion being the 1973 Skylab mission.

Where will the game go in the next ten years? There is a growing chorus suggesting that it might have already gone too far. I believe that whilst darts has not yet gone too far it is certainly moving in the wrong direction. There are a number of reasons for thinking that this is so.

Firstly, the idea of starting on a double has generally been dropped from major events so that a game of 501 can become a quick race down to the climax of the finishing double. In the process not only has an integral element of skill been lost but the game at this level now consists solely of two players plugging away at the treble twenty until it is time to get an odd number

125

and a double at the end. Such matches are played as the best of three, five, seven or whatever with the player starting the first game being decided by the toss of a coin; the result is that with two players of the calibre of, say, John Lowe and Eric Bristow, they rattle off the tons until the player who started gets down to the double first and so out. Consequently, he who wins the first leg wins the match.

Secondly, and this follows on from the first reason, the game is also becoming more boring to watch as the hockey inches closer and closer to the board. In recent years top class events have been played from a throwing distance of 7ft 6in and it is rare to see a game at this level with any shot below 60 in it. In fact, it is not uncommon to see a game with no shot below 100 in it, and at least one 180! In the days of Jim Pike, Joe Hitchcock and the other true giants of the game, a maximum shot of 180 was an event for lesser players to marvel at; it was not quite on a par with a 147 break in snooker but not far off it. Now the bulky brass darts have given way to slim tungsten ones and the old 9ft hockey is just an obsolete line on the mat a good way behind the thrower. Their darts *had* to be heavy to carry that distance. The way things are going today, if some of the basketball players I have seen ever took up darts we should be able to enjoy the spectacle of them almost *placing* their arrows in the board! Darts evolved from and developed around the basic principle that high scores were difficult to achieve and very high scores almost impossible; to make things deliberately easier for the players, or to allow them to become so, is surely to devalue the game.

Thirdly, the increase in the number of televised events has been a major contributor to those changes in the game already outlined. Darts, like snooker, is an ideal sport for television presentation but whereas television has not been responsible for changing the rules of snooker, it has for darts. No one, as far as I am aware, has seriously advocated getting rid of half the red balls in snooker and enlarging the pockets to make for a quicker, higher scoring game; why then has the opening double been abolished in darts and the throwing distance cut? Recently there has been some discussion on the possibility of a time limit rule for a throw, again for the 'benefit' of television.

This would of course penalise those players who, quite legitimately, like to take their time over their darts. If slow, deliberate players can be accommodated in televised snooker, why not also in darts?

Fourthly, governing bodies and national tournaments appear to be proliferating. There should be only one 'World' champion at any one time and likewise only one 'British' champion, 'USA' champion, etc. At present these titles are bandied about, in various forms, with increasing frequency and are only devalued in the process. Similarly the various regulating bodies should get together, if not amalgamate, for the benefit of the game, not the officials, while it is still at an early stage of international development. Otherwise we shall see a repeat of what has happened in boxing where there are two international governing bodies.

Finally, sponsorship − this is surely the real reason why the game has changed its character so much over the last decade. At one time sponsors such as the *News of the World* newspaper were content to take second place to the game itself; today commercial considerations are supreme. Prize money has escalated rapidly and is now into thousands of pounds and dollars for individuals, not the total. The American Darts Organisation is already talking in terms of the $100,000 tournament. For that amount the sponsors want a big song and dance in return; if necessary rules and traditions built up over many years of the game are chopped and changed or simply swept away to make darts an eminently presentable product. Every year there are more major tournaments, greater television coverage, more prizes and titles to be won. But it also becomes more standardised, more artificial, and more boring. And this is the worst thing that could ever happen to it.

There are two glimmers of hope that suggest this trend is not irreversible. One is the lengthening of the throwing distance to 7ft 9¼in (2.37m) by the WDF although it is not evident what was wrong with the old 8ft 6in. It is not even a round figure in metric terms − but then what has metrication to do with darts? The other ray of hope is the introduction of a board by one of Britain's leading manufacturers with half-width double and treble beds. Although intended just for practice (an excellent idea in itself), why not adopt it as the standard board for international matches? Players in the north of England can justly claim that they have been playing on such boards for years.

Many people are tired of watching professional darts and seeing ton after ton going down on the scoreboard with clockwork regularity. The interest and stature of the game would be helped by deliberately making it more difficult and skillful than it is now by introducing a harder board and/or a longer throwing distance. Such a move would be bringing the game back closer to its original state and make it possible to marvel at brilliant play when the occasional 180 is scored.

One final point: the ordinary lunchtime and evening players do not need the glittering prizes, the big names, the commercialism of big-time darts. The way things are developing, professional darts may well be harmed or even killed by pulling it so far away from the real game. If that happens all we have to do is saunter down the road to the local, wander pint in hand over to the light in the corner with the smoke curling round it and put our name on the board. *That* is what darts is all about.

A darts glossary

Like any other game, darts has acquired its own language and terminology over the years. It is a feature of the game in its own right and for sheer number of words and obscurity of origin it surpasses most other pastimes. Listed below are some hundred or so terms peculiar to the game; for many of them I have no idea how or when they were introduced by players.

I have deliberately omitted terms borrowed from other games or contemporary slang since they cannot really be said to belong to darts and, in many cases, come and go with great rapidity. Good examples of these are bingo calls such as 'clickety-click' (66), 'legs eleven' (11) and so on. Now that bingo occupies its own clearly defined place in the world of games, its own language tends to be used there and there alone and has generally been dropped from darts.

Those terms marked with an asterisk are ones listed by Croft-Cooke which are not, as far as I am aware, in common usage – though there may well be particular localities where they are still going strong. I would like to think that they are for they certainly add to the fascinating richness of the game.

arrow   dart (Pronounced 'arrer' in the south)
away   in a position to score after the starting double has been hit
*bag o' nuts   a score of 45 (Berkshire)
barrel   the weighted section of a dart
bed   an indivisible section of the board such as any double or treble
bed and breakfast   a score of 26, traditionally made with 20, 5 and 1
*been   another term for **bust**
big   as in 'big 6': the larger of the two single beds of a number
big girls' board   derogatory nickname by Manchester board players for the London variety
*Bill Harvey   a score of 100
*Bill Taylor   1
*blacking back!   one of numerous calls to the thrower to move his feet behind the hockey
bombers   extremely heavy darts
*brewer   another term for **bed and breakfast**
brush   as in 'We gave them the brush': to win without the other side scoring

bull   the 25 and 50 circles on double bull boards or the 50 on single bull boards

***bull calf**   a score of 33 (Gloucester)

bull out   to be out on the bull

bull's eye   the 50 circle

bull-up (or **off**)   to throw for the bull to decide who starts the game

bust   scored too many

cannons   another term for **bombers**

***cat's on the counter!**   a call by the winners to the losers to stand them a drink

chalk   to keep score, usually in order to challenge the winner

come out!   a call to a player to stop throwing as he is bust

cracked   when a single of a number is scored in place of the attempted double

dead   as in '12 dead' – exactly

dead bull   another term for the **bull's eye**

downstairs   the lower section of the board

double Nelson   a score of 222 (See **Nelson**)

double top   20x ('Top' is not normally used on its own)

***dry-wipe**   first two legs of a three-leg match won

***father's boots!**   another term for **blacking back!** – the sarcastic question: 'Got your dad's big boots on, then?'

game on!   a call for quiet during play

game shot   a shot to win the game

getting out   making a **game shot**

getting the odd (or **one**) **off**   eg getting 1 off 9 to leave 4x

going back   reverting to an earlier score after **going bust**

going bust   scoring too many

good arrows   term of congratulation for a particularly useful throw

granny   intriguing Scottish term for the **brush**

half-a-crown   another term for **bed and breakfast,** dating back a long long way to when the one cost the other!

hitting the woodwork   a shot off the board completely

hockey   the throwing mark

***hops!**   another term for **cat's on the counter!**

***in the wilderness**   99 left

island   as in 'off the island' – the scoring area of the board

leg   one game of several in a match (usually three or five)

leg-and-leg   both teams have won one **leg**

level pegging (or **pegs**)   equal scoring (A reference to crib board scoring)

levelling-up   allowing the loser the same number of darts as the winner of a game

little ` as in 'little 6': the smaller of the two single beds of a number
little Audrey   the bull (Lancashire)
Lord Nelson   see **Nelson**
*Lord Sherbourne   a score of 33. Apparently a certain peer of this title used this number as his car's registration (Cotswolds)
madhouse   1x
marker   1) the scorer   2) a dart close to the required number used to line up the next dart
married man's side   the left-hand side of the board – the safe side avoiding very low (and high) scores
middle-for-diddle   another term for **bull-up**
move across   to aim across the board from the last number thrown
mugs away!   a call for the losers to go first in a return game
nails   extremely thin darts virtually the same width all the way down
nearest and furthest   when four players throw for the **bull** to select partners for a doubles game. Nearest and furthest play against the middle pair
Nelson   a score of 111. From the saying 'One eye, one arm, one . . .' (use your own imagination)
never won a game   superstition that a player left with a certain number (usually 99 or 123) will not win
no practising!   another term for **come out!**
off   another term for **away**
*office!   call when **game shot** is achieved
*old lady!   another term for **office!** (Home Counties)
on   as in 'We're on': turn to play a game
one foot (or **toe**) **in the water**   overstepping the **hockey**
out   a dart landing just over the wire from the required number
*Oxo   a score of 0
pegger   the scorer (Another reference to crib board scoring)
*pug   the **bull** (Sussex)
puncture   hitting the tyre (if there is one) around the board
put one up (for the bull)   another term for **bull-up**
quadrant   geometrically incorrect term for a segment of the board composed of two adjacent numbers eg the 10–15 quadrant
rough   as in '3 rough' – a low, odd score left at the end of a throw
*scorer's dry!   a call from the scorer that, the scores being level, he ought to be stood a drink!
sergeant   used in the game Round the Board – scoring three successive numbers in the three darts of a throw to win a free turn
*setting   the first player to **bull-up**, 'sets' his opponent
Shanghai   three darts in the same number in the single, double and treble beds

soldiers   another term for **sergeant**

spider (or, more correctly, **spider's web**)   the wire assembly marking out the **beds**

split   another term for **cracked**

splitting the eleven   landing a dart in the centre of the wire numeral 11

strike   a player about to throw is said to 'have the strike'

*Style and Winch   yet another term for 26. (The name of a brewery firm)

switching   giving up going for one number and trying for another

three for it   throwing for 1x at the end of a long game, ignoring anything else scored

three in a bed   three darts landed in the same **bed**

three in a row   another term for a **sergeant**

three up   a practice throw of three darts before a game

tin hat   another term for the **brush**

ton   a score of 100

top of the house (or **shop**)   another term for 20x

tops   another term for 20x

turf   another term for **island**

two-and-six   another term for 26 (ie half-a-crown in old money)

up in Annie's room   another term for 1x

upstairs   the upper section of the board

*waggon and horses   yet another term for 1x

*weaver's donkey   a score of 42 (Berkshire)

whitewash   another term for the **brush**

win the toss, lose the game   darts proverb

wiring one   bouncing a dart off the wire or landing it next to the wire

Appendix 1

Leading darts bodies in the British Isles

NATIONAL DARTS ASSOCIATION OF GREAT BRITAIN
General Secretary: Charles Burden, 'Trevan', Trevanion Road, Wadebridge, Cornwall.

CLUB AND INSTITUTE UNION
Club Union House, 251/256 Upper Street, London N1

BRITISH DARTS ORGANISATION
General Secretary: Olly Croft, 47 Creighton Avenue, Muswell Hill, London N10

ENGLAND DARTS ORGANISATION
As above. (Affiliated to the WDF.)

SCOTTISH DARTS ASSOCIATION
General Secretary: Tom Frost, 17 Struan Drive, Inverkeithing, Fife. (Affiliated to the WDF.)

WELSH DARTS ORGANISATION
General Secretary: Allan Clark, Royal Oak Hotel, Henfaes Road, Tonna, Neath. (Affiliated to the WDF.)

IRISH DARTS ORGANISATION
General Secretary: Louis Donohoe, Kings Inn Bar, 42 Bolton Street, Dublin, Eire. (Affiliated to the WDF.)

ULSTER FEDERATION OF DARTS
General Secretary: Hugh Ennis, 58 Sandown Road, Belfast, N. Ireland

WORLD DARTS FEDERATION
General Secretary: Olly Croft, 47 Creighton Avenue, Muswell Hill, London N10

Appendix 2

Leading darts bodies overseas

AUSTRALIA
A. R. Singleton, Australian Darts Council Inc, 76 Hampton Circuit, Yarralumla, ACT 2600, Australia*

BARBADOS
Barbados Darts Association, c/o Barbados Light & Power Co, The Garrison, St Michaels, Barbados

BELGIUM
Roger Vannoorden, Fédération Belgique de Dards, 14 Beek Straat, 8600 Menen, Belgium*

BERMUDA
M. J. Tavares, Bermuda Darts Organisation, PO Box 207, Hamilton 5, Bermuda*

CANADA
Ron Steggal, National Darts Association of Canada, PO Box 13, Station M, Toronto, Ontario, Canada*

DENMARK
P. S. Schultz, Dansk Dart Union, Lundemogen 106, 2670 Greve Strand, Denmark*

FIJI
Fiji Darts Association, PO Box 59, Suva, Fiji Islands

FINLAND
Kari Hintikka, Finnish Darts Union, Jaakarink 10A6, 00150, Helsinki 15, Finland*

FRANCE
Fédération Française de Dards, 142 Rue des Landes, 78400 Chatou, France*

GIBRALTAR

Gibraltar Darts Association, c/o Odd Fellows Club, 3 Victualling Office Lane, Gibraltar*

GUYANA

c/o Grantly Culbard, CC Workers Union, 140 Murray Street, PO Box 780, Georgetown, Guyana, West Indies

HONG KONG

Tom Smith, Hong Kong Darts Association, c/o The China Fleet Club, Gloucester Road, Wanchai, Hong Kong*

JAMAICA

Friendly Darts League, 5 Ridgefield Avenue, Kingston 8, Jamaica

JAPAN

B. R. Brick, Nipon Darts Kyoka, 2-26-22 Denenchofu, Ota-Ku, Tokyo, Japan*

MALTA

Louis Florian, Malta Darts Association, St Rita Luqua Road, Pawla, Malta*

NETHERLANDS

Colin Brown, Nederlandse Darts Bond, Post Box 16290 Den Haag, Holland*

NEW ZEALAND

I. M. Frazer, New Zealand Darts Council Inc, PO Box 767, Nelson, New Zealand*

SOUTH AFRICA

S. N. Bam, South African Darts Association, 81 Da Gama Street, Strand 7140, Cape Province, South Africa*

SWEDEN

K. Seagran, Svenska Dartforbundet, Box 137, 772 Ozgrangesberg, Sweden*

TRINIDAD

South Trinidad Darts Association, c/o George Simpson, Texaco (Trinidad Inc), Pointe-A-Pierre, Trinidad, West Indies

USA

Tom Fleetwood, American Darts Organisation, 13841 Eastbrook Avenue, Bellflower, California 90706, USA*

* affiliated to the WDF

Appendix 3

News of the World Championship winners

LONDON
1928	Sammy Stone	1932	J. R. Hood
1929	J. Hoare	1933	H. Enever
1930	C. Bowley	1934	F. Metson
1931	T. Nye	1935	W. Forecast

LONDON & HOME COUNTIES
1936	Peter Finnigan	1938	F. A. Wallis
1937	Stan Outten		

LONDON & SOUTH OF ENGLAND
1939 Marmaduke Breckon

LANCASHIRE & CHESHIRE
1938	W. McIntosh	1939	P. Birchall

MIDLAND COUNTIES
1939 H. Prior

NORTH OF ENGLAND
1939 J. Young

YORKSHIRE
1939 J. Munroe

WALES
1937	D. Cornacia	1939	C. Parker
1938	G. Jones		

ENGLAND & WALES
1948	Harry Leadbetter	1960	Tom Reddington
1949	Jackie Boyce	1961	Alec Adamson
1950	Dixie Newberry	1962	Eddie Brown
1951	Harry Perryman	1963	Robbie Rumney
1952	Tommy Gibbons	1964	Tom Barrett
1953	Jimmy Carr	1965	Tom Barrett
1954	Oliver James	1966	Wilf Ellis
1955	Tom Reddington	1967	Wally Seaton
1956	Trevor Peachey	1968	Bill Duddy
1957	Alwyn Mullins	1969	Barry Twomlow
1958	Tommy Gibbons	1970	Henry Barney
1959	Albert Welch	1971	Dennis Filkins

ENGLAND, WALES & SCOTLAND

1972	Brian Netherton	1976	Billy Lennard
1973	Ivor Hodgkinson	1977	Mick Norris
1974	Peter Chapman	1978	Stefan Lord*
1975	Derek 'Chalky' White	1979	Bobby George

* From Sweden: see Chapter 11 for the development of the tournament to the international level.

Bibliography

Very little exists in the way of literature dealing solely with the game – and of those books that do all but one have been written in the last ten years. The same holds true for the coverage of pub games in general.

On darts

Croft-Cooke, Rupert, *Darts* Geoffrey Bles, London, 1936
  My views on this book have been stated in Chapter 10; it is however important as the first book entirely devoted to the game.
Williamson, Noel Egbert, *Darts* Elliot Right Way Books, Kingswood, 1968
  A 'popular' paperback approach to the game that is really no more informative than the above book by Croft-Cooke.
Barrett, Tom, *Darts* Pan, London, 1973
  Another paperback but this time of much greater value. The early history of the game is dealt with extremely briefly but the coverage of the period from the 1930s onwards is good. More of an autobiography than a book on the game itself.
Brown, Derek, *Darts* 'Know the game' Series EP Publishing, Wakefield, 1978
  A good, concise introduction to all aspects of the game.

On pub games

Finn, Timothy, *The Watney book of pub games* Queen Anne Press, London, 1966
—— *Pub games of England* Queen Anne Press, London, 1975
  Although rather lightweight in content the Watney's book is of historical importance as the first attempt to systematically cover this field. The later book is much more comprehensive and far better illustrated.
Inn games 'Know the game' Series EP Publishing, Wakefield, reissued 1973
  A basic how-to-play-them booklet.
Taylor, Arthur R., *Pub games* Mayflower Books, St Albans, 1976
  Another paperback book on the subject but totally different from the previous one with its 256 pages packed with information and diagrams. The darts section is particularly good.

Of background relevance

Francis, Rev. P. H., *A study of targets in games* Mitre Press, London, 1951

Trench, Charles Chenevix, *A history of marksmanship* Longman, London, 1972

Heath, E. G., *A history of target archery* David & Charles, Newton Abbot, 1973

Hardy, Robert, *Longbow* Patrick Stephens, Cambridge, 1976
These books I have found of special value whilst researching the origins and history of the game.

Periodicals

Darts World
A glossy monthly magazine which provides complete coverage of events in the darts world, major match results, trade advertisements and so on. A must for any serious British player.

Yearbooks

Information on forthcoming fixtures, title holders, recent championships, personalities etc can be found in the yearbooks which have recently begun to appear as the status of darts has increased. At the time of writing the principal British ones available are:

Brown, Derek, *Darts '78* Mirror Books Ltd, London

Elkadart International Darts Handbook International Darts Handbook Information Centre

Leighton Rees Darts Yearbook Billboard Ltd, London

Unicorn Darts Yearbook Studio Publications, Ipswich
In addition, both the BDO and the NDAGB publish their own handbook; the same holds true for their counterparts overseas.

Other sources consulted but not mentioned here are either noted at the appropriate point in the text or are merely basic reference works which, in the majority of cases, provided the odd item of background information but nothing on the game.

Acknowledgements

I should like to express my gratitude to all those who have so willingly helped me during the writing of this book. I am especially grateful to the following firms and individuals: Kwiz Darts Ltd; Nodor Co Ltd; Unicorn Products Ltd; 'Winmau' Dartboard Co Ltd; George Oliver, Head Librarian at the *News of the World*; Olly Croft of the BDO and WDF; Arthur R. Singleton, President of the Darts Federation of Australia; Bill Turner, Vice-President of the New Zealand Darts Council and Tom Fleetwood, Secretary of the American Darts Organisation. And to Sue, but for whose every encouragement it might never have been written: thank you.

Special thanks must also go to John Henry for his excellent drawings which have admirably enhanced the text and also to Tony Brown for his invaluable tips and advice on winning play.

Last – and by no means least – I should like to thank all those throughout Britain who have, over the years, given me so many happy hours in front of unnumerable dartboards.